Post Traumatic Stress Disorder: the invisible injury, 2005 edition is a revised and updated version of the 1998 and 2001 editions of David Kinchin's book, originally published in 1994 with the title *Post Traumatic Stress Disorder: a practical guide to recovery.* The 2005 edition contains a revised chapter examining Critical Incident Stress Debriefing.

David Kinchin's research is at the forefront of identifying, understanding and addressing the causes of trauma, stress and psychiatric injury. *Post Traumatic Stress Disorder: the invisible injury, 2005 edition* remains a leader in its field.

Post Traumatic Stress Disorder

THE INVISIBLE INJURY

2005 EDITION

David Kinchin

Success
Unlimited

2004

Published in Great Britain in 2004

Success Unlimited
PO Box 67, Didcot, Oxfordshire OX11 9YS, UK

British Library Cataloguing in Publication Data
A catalogue record for this book is
available from the British Library.

ISBN 0 9529121 47

Typeset using FrameMaker® in Helvetica 10 point.

All brand or product names are trademarks or registered
trademarks of their respective companies or organizations.

Printed in Great Britain by
Wessex Press, Wantage, Oxfordshire.

Post Traumatic Stress Disorder: the invisible injury, 2005 edition

by

David Kinchin

Contents

Introduction

On Saturday 14 July 1990 I was busy at work as a police officer with the traffic department of Thames Valley Police. I had been a police officer for 11 years. My wife and three children were happy with my career and I had nearly always managed to leave my work behind me when I went off duty. The following day, what started off as a routine evening's work ended when I found myself in the centre of a riot. I was surrounded by angry, hostile faces without another police uniform in sight. I was kicked, punched, spat upon and sworn at. I was trapped. For a few terrifying minutes I thought I was going to die.

I had watched other people come to terms with traumatic events, but this was the first time that I had experienced a serious, potentially life-threatening situation myself. I was admitted to hospital with a broken cheekbone and damage to my kidneys and spleen. In the weeks that followed I was also diagnosed as suffering from Post Traumatic Stress Disorder (PTSD).

I had never heard of Post Traumatic Stress Disorder and I wanted to find out more. I wanted to meet other people who had been similarly diagnosed. This was not easy. Almost all texts on the subject had been written by medical experts and academics for peer readership, and trying to find other sufferers to compare notes with was rather like an agoraphobic trying to find another sufferer to talk to. I knew that there must be hundreds around but I didn't know how to contact them.

Eventually I did find other people who were suffering from Post Traumatic Stress Disorder. A few were fellow police officers, but most were just people who had been unfortunate in finding themselves unexpectedly involved in an extremely traumatic incident and who thought they were going to die. As a result of sharing my ideas with many of these people, I decided that I had to write my own book. In the book I would include my own story and the stories of several other PTSD sufferers. The book would be written by a PTSD sufferer, for other PTSD sufferers. The book was published by Thorsons under the title *Post Traumatic Stress Disorder: a practical guide to recovery* in September 1994, a shade over four years after my assault.

Another four years passed and it was clear that the book needed revising and updating. Those who read the original volume were complimentary about the straightforward language and how easy it was to understand the text. I received hundreds of letters from PTSD sufferers who gained hope from reading my book.

Time passed, and all the original copies of 'practical guide' sold out. It was time to update the book again. Whilst being delighted that my books have proved so popular, particularly with those at the receiving end of PTSD, I remained saddened that in the time since the publication of my first book in 1994, there have been few advances in the recognition of PTSD and in the treatment of the disorder within the UK health service. At the time of revising this book (July 2004) there is not a single NHS bed in UK set aside for the treatment of PTSD. That can't be right!

On 31 August 1997 the world was distressed to hear of the sudden death of Diana, Princess of Wales. The horror of the Paris car crash in which she died affected millions of ordinary people all around the world. Many were affected by the trauma of this event simply because they knew that a beautiful young woman had died in appallingly traumatic circumstances. If we can all be so deeply moved by the death of a well-loved public figure then there can be little doubt that we are all susceptible to the effects of trauma when they strike our own family and friends.

The 2001 edition was brought up to date for the new millennium. The idea of Complex PTSD was introduced and The Snakes and Ladders Model of Recovery was expanded. I strongly believe this remains the most realistic Recovery Model to be published to date. Indeed, most texts ignore recovery altogether. For the 2005 edition Chapter 12 Early Interventions (Debriefing) was revised and updated.

Having checked all the obvious catalogues, I am convinced this remains the only book written by a PTSD sufferer, for fellow PTSD sufferers.

This is the book I so badly wanted to read when I was traumatised.

David Kinchin
Oxfordshire, July 2004

Please Listen

When I ask you to listen to me
and you start giving advice you have
not done what I asked.

When I ask you to listen to me
and you begin to tell me why I
shouldn't feel that way you are
trampling on my feelings.

When I ask you to listen to me
and you feel you have to do something
to solve my problems you have failed me,
strange as it may seem.

When you do something for me that I
can and need to do for myself,
you contribute to my fear and weakness.

So,
please listen and just hear me,
and, if you want to talk,
wait a minute for your turn: and I will listen to you.

Anonymous

Chapter one

What is Post Traumatic Stress Disorder?

09.15 *School's settled down. Teacher is about to mark the register. A call of 'dinner children' from the corridor. Some go to pay their dinner shillings in the hall. Two are spotted by the headmistress, Miss Jennings, and sent to the senior school with a message.*

09.18 *An avalanche crashes through the school. It kills one of the two children on their way to the senior school. A black, wet mass slurps through a classroom, and fills Miss Jennings's study. She's 64, due to retire at the end of term. Next door to her Mrs Bates and 33 children, aged 10 and 11, all die.*

09.29 *All 11 of the school soccer team, who had won 3-2 the afternoon before, are killed.*

If this were fiction it would be horrifying enough, but the fact that it actually happened gives it a traumatic quality. We live in an age when such events seem to occur with ever-increasing frequency. Not a single day passes without a calamity affecting some part of the planet, and pictures of these events are immediately flashed to our TV screens and our newspapers. The disadvantage of having such an efficient and prompt news service is that everyone becomes better acquainted with the dangers life may have in store. We are all more traumatically cognisant.

Apart from headline-making disasters, there are other sources of trauma. All around, people become victims of crime and accidents, quite often with devastating consequences. Many of these events go unnoticed except for the few people who have been directly affected by such ordeals, but many of the victims may later suffer from Post Traumatic Stress Disorder (PTSD).

Trauma is defined in the Oxford English Dictionary as 'a powerful shock that may have long-lasting consequences'. The effects of trauma can be immediately overwhelming.

PTSD results when a person has been exposed to an event which is outside the range of normal human experience: an event which would markedly distress almost anyone. It is the normal human response to an abnormal situation. The experience could be a serious threat to life. It could be a serious threat or actual harm to one's children, partner or other close relative or friend. It could be the sudden destruction of one's home or community, or seeing another person who has recently been seriously injured or killed as the result of either an accident or physical violence.

PTSD goes further. The event only has to be perceived as traumatic by the victim. In reality the incident might not pose a serious threat to life, but if the incident is genuinely considered to be life-threatening, then the victim has experienced an event outside the range of normal human experience. More recent evidence has shown that PTSD can result from sexual abuse, and from bullying.

I believe that the increase in PTSD is very much the product of modern living. PTSD case numbers rise in ratio to advances in technology. The more advanced today's world becomes, the greater the scope for the existence of severe life stresses and traumatic situations. The more advanced our communications networks become, the more our minds are filled with plausible traumatic imagery. I suspect the incidence of PTSD cases will continue to rise.

Large-scale disasters, either natural or man-made, will inevitably lead to a large number of people within one community being affected by PTSD. On 21 October 1966 a waste tip from a Welsh coal field slid down the side of a valley and demolished several houses and a village school. The incident at Aberfan killed 116 children and 28 adults (Austin 1967). The opening paragraph of this chapter describes part of this disaster. In less than twenty minutes every person in that community had been permanently scarred by a disaster which touched the hearts of millions.

This disaster is vividly recalled by many Britons because it was covered by television crews who arrived on the scene within hours. The full horror and traumatic consequences of the disaster were screened in millions of homes.

Five-and-a-half years later, a similar event happened in the USA. On 26 February 1972 an enormous slag dam gave way and unleashed thousands of tonnes of water on the communities of Buffalo Creek, West Virginia. The mining hamlets of Becco, Lundale and Pardee were almost totally destroyed (Erikson 1976). The disaster resulted in 126 deaths, and it left 4,000 people homeless. Like the Aberfan tragedy, the actual incident lasted less than twenty minutes, but the consequences were devastating.

In 1966 the people of Aberfan were considered to be suffering from 'severe shock'. In 1972 those in Buffalo Creek were labelled as suffering from a complex which became journalistically known as 'Buffalo Creek Syndrome'.

After seeing so many traumatised Vietnam veterans, the medical profession recognised that all victims of extremely traumatic events tended to exhibit similar behaviour and symptoms. Significant numbers of Vietnam veterans were displaying signs that all was not well with their lives. Their traumatic wartime experiences were adversely affecting their state of health. Upon returning home they were not welcomed as heroes. Civilians just did not want to know. The combination of suffering severe trauma and experiencing such a negative reaction back home led some veterans to resort to drink, drugs and violence.

In 1980 the symptoms exhibited by these veterans, and those exhibited by civilian victims such as those who suffered at Buffalo Creek, were grouped under the diagnosis of Post Traumatic Stress Disorder. The definition, coded DSM-III, gave a name to the disorder and officially replaced such terms as: shell shock (1940); gross stress reaction (1952); transient situation disturbance (1968); and Buffalo Creek Syndrome (1972).

In 1994 this definition was amended once more (DSM-IV) and is now recognised world-wide.

In the wake of the terrorist act which caused the Lockerbie plane crash, many of the rescue workers struggled to cope with the horrific scenes before their eyes. By the date of the disaster, 21 December 1988, it was readily acknowledged that these people were likely to develop symptoms of Post Traumatic Stress Disorder.

Much more recently, the shooting incident in Dunblane shocked even the most hardened people. How it was possible for one man to walk into a school and shoot dead sixteen children was hard to imagine. But that is exactly what 43-year-old Thomas Hamilton did on 13 March 1996. The world was deeply scandalised by yet another incident that lasted less than twenty minutes. The shock waves following this event lasted a long time. Britain, and the world, was becoming more aware of what traumatic events can do to individual people, to families and to communities. By the time of the Dunblane shootings everyone was at least familiar with the initials PTSD even if they did not fully understand the disorder.

This tragic shooting provided the largest incidence of "trauma bonding". In particular, there developed a bond between the residents of Dunblane and those living in Aberfan. The two disasters were separated by thirty years and about 315 miles of countryside, but the two communities were united by an invisible "trauma bond". This bond is an invisible understanding which exists between those who have witnessed or experienced a traumatic event.

Set out in table form, the criteria for establishing PTSD appear cold and clinical. Examples used later will add a considerable degree of reality to the disorder and make these symptoms more understandable.

HOW MANY PEOPLE SUFFER FROM PTSD?

The number of people who suffer from PTSD at any one time is equal to about one per cent of the general population. In 1987 researchers carried out a survey of psychological disorders exhibited by the population of St Louis, Missouri (Helzer 1987). A total of 2,500 randomly selected residents was studied, and 28

Six criteria need to be met before a diagnosis of Post Traumatic Stress Disorder can be made (DSM-IV) (Kinchin 1998)

1 TRAUMA   The person must be exposed to a traumatic event or events that involve actual or threatened death or serious injury, or threat to the physical integrity of self or others. The person's response must involve fear, helplessness or horror.
2 INTRUSIVE The event must be persistently relived by the person.
3 AVOIDANT The person must persistently avoid stimuli associated with the trauma.
4 PHYSICAL The person must experience persistent symptoms of increased arousal, or 'over-awareness'.
5 SOCIAL   The disturbance must cause significant distress or impairment in social, occupational, or other areas of functioning important to the person.
6 TIME   Symptoms, linked to 2, 3 and 4 above, must have lasted at least a month.

people were diagnosed as suffering from PTSD. Of those 28, the men cited only two types of event as a cause of the disorder: combat and witnessing someone hurt or die. The most common event cited by the women was physical attack, including rape. Other events which were identified as triggering PTSD were being poisoned, and having a miscarriage. Major disasters accounted for none of the 28 cases. Within some groups of society, the incidence of PTSD must be expected to be much higher than one per cent. Within the emergency services (fire, police and ambulance) and the armed forces (army, navy and air force) the incidence of PTSD can be as high as 15 per cent (Ravenscroft 1993). It is a disturbing probability that out of every hundred police officers currently engaged in uniformed patrol duties in our towns and cities, fifteen will be suffering from symptoms in accord with PTSD.

As with every other subject, Post Traumatic Stress has its own statistics to quote. Much of the work on the subject was brought about by the so-called "Disaster era" between 1985 and 1989. During those five years, thirteen major incidents shook

Britain killing over one thousand people and traumatising many more.

These major incidents claimed considerable media attention and rightly so. But the only figures produced after each incident referred to fatalities. Without wishing to trivialise any death, it is true to say that dead people do not suffer from Post Traumatic Stress Disorder. However, those who saw them die, or who were close to them either emotionally or physically at the time of their death, may well develop symptoms of PTSD. It is generally estimated that for every one death in an incident, there are likely to be at least eight people who are traumatised and go on to develop PTSD. So the thirteen disasters cited in the UK disaster era may well have produced around 8,500 cases of PTSD.

The UK disaster era: 1985-1989		
Date	**Event**	**Deaths**
12 May 1985	Bradford City Football stadium fire	40
29 May 1985	Heysel Stadium crowd disturbance	56
22 Aug 1985	Manchester Airport fire	55
6 Mar 1987	Herald of Free Enterprise sank	187
19 Aug 1987	Hungerford shootings	16
11 Nov 1987	Enniskillen bombing	12
18 Nov 1987	King's Cross fire	31
6 Jul 1988	Piper Alpha oil rig fire	167
12 Dec 1988	Clapham rail crash	35
21 Dec 1988	Lockerbie plane crash	270
8 Jan 1989	East Midlands plane crash	47
15 Apr 1989	Hillsborough Stadium disaster	96
20 Aug 1989	Marchioness pleasure boat sank	51
	Total	1,063

But, major disasters account for only a fraction of the number of people who die as a result of accidents or violence.

Total UK deaths from accidents and violence: 1985-1989					
	1985	**1986**	**1987**	**1988**	**1989**
(a) Total figure	22,564	22,389	21,271	21,634	21,004
(b) Disasters	151	0	246	472	194
(b) as % of (a)	0.7%	0.0%	1.2%	2.2%	0.9%

During the five years of 1985 to 1989 there were 108,862 fatalities of which just 1,063 were linked to the thirteen well-publicised major disasters. The rest of the fatalities are made up from car accidents, domestic accidents, crimes of violence and all the other incidents which account for about 56 deaths every day in UK and which pass almost unnoticed by many of us. If the "eight for one rule" is applied to all these deaths, that is, eight cases of PTSD for every fatality, then over 870,000 people suffered from PTSD in Britain during that same five-year period. This figure is equal to 1.5% of the total population.

Post Traumatic Stress Disorder high-risk groups	
Event	**Risk**
Shipwreck survivors	75%
Bombing (terrorism) survivors	50%
Sexual abuse victims	50%
Rape victims	50%
Combat victims	40%
Hijack survivors	35%
Victims of bullying	35%
Air crash survivors	25%
Car crash victims	20%
Emergency service staff	15%
GENERAL POPULATION	1.5%

Of course, the "eight for one rule" cannot be applied rigidly. But it can be used as a general guide. Any attempt to calculate more accurate figures would have to take into account that some events are more likely to traumatise people than others. For example, rape victims have a 50% risk of suffering PTSD following their ordeal while car crash victims have only a 20% chance. In addition, it would appear that some people may be more susceptible to PTSD than others, although there is no official agreement on this issue. These variables all have to be considered.

The generally agreed figure for the number of cases of PTSD within the population is 1.5%.

In some instances, the individual may have experienced a prolonged series of stressful circumstances. A Vietnam veteran may have experienced several traumatic combat incidents over a period of weeks or months. A fire officer may deal with a run of house fires in which children have been fatally burned. In cases like these, the extensive cumulative stress can result in Prolonged Duress Stress Disorder (PDSD) which results in the same symptoms as PTSD. PDSD is now more frequently referred to as 'Complex PTSD' by many commentators.

Complex Post Traumatic Stress Disorder may be experienced by some unlikely victims. For example, Dr Iain West is Britain's leading forensic pathologist. He experiences on a daily basis sights that most people would find physically and emotionally abhorrent. His job is to carry out physical examinations of victims of fatal crimes, or accidents. He led investigating teams to deal with the aftermath of the Hillsborough, King's Cross and Clapham disasters. Dr West has also been deeply involved with cases of suicide, murder and child abuse. Following the case of baby Tyra Henry, a twenty-one-month-old infant who was dropped in a fight between her parents, Dr West was quoted (Stern 1996) as saying,

"The examinations of both Jasmine (Tyra's sister) and Tyra have left images that I will always have in my mind - the state of their little bodies the first time I saw them. I will never forget them."

Perhaps someone in this position is likely to become a victim of Complex PTSD.

IS WHAT I AM EXPERIENCING NORMAL?

There are over 6,000 million people on this planet. Consequently, there are the same number of different reactions to any situation. No two people will have an identical reaction to one event. That is what makes us human. Two people who experience the same event together will react to it differently. If there are two hundred people present, the variety of reactions is multiplied by that number, the only difference in a large group is that several people may have broadly similar reactions. Confronted by a traumatic situation some will face it, others will move away. This reaction is referred to as 'fight or flight'. If the event is particularly traumatic, many will run the risk of developing PTSD.

Who can say what is normal? What can be said, without fear of contradiction, is that a person who is faced with an abnormal situation will react in some way to that situation. How the person reacts will depend on many other factors, such as previous experiences, mood at the time of the event, and individual perception of the threat to personal safety.

Suppose you are leaving the cinema one evening and you come face to face with a youth. He waves a sharp knife under your nose and demands all your cash. It is likely that you first feel fear, then anger, then logic takes over and you reason no amount of cash is worth a slashed face. The youth grins wildly, waves your money under your gaze to signify his victory, and runs off.

If, three weeks later, you are leaving a cinema and someone rushes up to you brandishing your forgotten coat, your first reaction is one of panic. Your mind, briefly, links the two events because some aspects of the first traumatic event have been repeated in the second, friendly, incident. Most people familiar with the circumstances of the robbery will see your initial panic reaction as normal. People witnessing the second event, not knowing about the robbery, might consider your initial panic as rather unusual. It is all a matter of perception and understanding.

Radiation is widely perceived as a threat to life. Few of us fully understand it or can visualise it, but we all know it can kill. In

March 1979 there was a radiation 'incident' at Three Mile Island in America.

Three Mile Island is situated near Harrisburg, Pennsylvania. The incident was contained within the power station complex. There was no real risk to the residents of the town. However, only a few months before that incident, a film describing a fictional nuclear accident had been released. The China Syndrome, starring Jane Fonda, told the story of a negligent power company searching for greater profits at the expense of safety. The result was the ultimate nightmare of a nuclear meltdown.

The nuclear lobby rubbished The China Syndrome as alarmist. However, at Three Mile Island, Hollywood drama was being acted out in real life. Naturally, people's perceptions of the risks involved had been altered by the film. There were no fatalities in Pennsylvania, but large numbers of people panicked and became severely traumatised by the incident. In the circumstances, this panic was both normal and reasonable.

The situation was to be repeated in 1986, this time at Chernobyl in Russia. The consequences on that occasion were far more devastating.

AM I GOING MAD?

Post Traumatic Stress Disorder is a psychological phenomenon. It is an emotional condition, from which it is possible to make a full and complete recovery.

The most distressing symptom of PTSD is the reliving of the traumatic event, whether you want to or not. This re-experiencing may take the form of recurrent nightmares, or daytime flashbacks. In either case you are troubled by vivid, repetitive pictures of the trauma. Sometimes these pictures are so real that you start to behave as though the event is happening all over again. This re-experiencing may last only a few seconds, but it might last hours or even days initially. Often you are fully aware of what is happening but can do nothing to control the situation. The flashbacks can occur with distressing frequency, adding fuel to the erroneous belief that you are 'going mad'.

The memory of the event is usually in picture form. Sounds and smells can act as a trigger to start the picture sequence. Former Middle East hostage, Terry Waite, tells how the sound of ripping masking tape triggered terrible memories of his days in captivity (Waite 1993). Chained and blindfolded in a tiny cell, he was frequently moved from one 'safe house' to another. Before every move he was bound with masking tape; even his mouth and eyes were covered. It is little wonder that a harmless and familiar sound to many should be such a traumatic trigger for him.

Because these vivid flashbacks are so unpredictable, victims find themselves at a disadvantage. Former friends and colleagues may feel insecure and unsure about how to react. Canteen chatterers may start to label the victim as a 'nutter' or a 'head case'. These labels are not appropriate to anyone, and they are certainly not appropriate descriptions of a PTSD victim. Unfortunately, the labels tend to stick. Victims start to panic. They avoid situations or activities which are likely to trigger the images. Their lifestyle changes and they start to lose contact with other people.

This spiral of events may lead to feelings of depression and anxiety. Untreated, this can have dangerous and far-reaching consequences. Resultant poor attendance at the workplace may result in unemployment, and irritability often adds strain to all personal relationships. All this, combined with possible uncontrollable and violent outbursts during periods when the victim is re-experiencing the trauma, can add up to an unbearable life. Things cannot continue in this way for long.

In seeking medical help, the last straw for PTSD victims is to picture themselves as mentally irredeemable cases doomed to spend the rest of their lives in a Dickensian-style institution for the insane.

This is a false expectation, but one common to many PTSD sufferers. They are not mad, but they do require specialised help.

WHY ME?

If every person who ever experienced a traumatic event always suffered from PTSD, the disorder would become almost as common as colds or flu. Clearly not everyone is affected to that same degree. Why?

Research studies that have examined the causes of PTSD are scarce. It is still difficult to identify those most likely to be affected, and those at greatest risk. Very little of the research is conclusive and any figures quoting a person's 'PTSD risk' are likely to be contested by various bodies having a vested interest in either underestimating or overestimating the figures. Defence departments will play down the figures. When asked about PTSD cases in 1994, the Ministry of Defence in London claimed that only 68 British combat troops received any form of psychiatric treatment as a direct result of the Gulf War. The independent group, TACT (the Trauma After Care Trust), claimed that the figure to be at least 13,000. The reality has proved to be far worse than either of these early predictions.

First it is necessary to look at the groups of people likely to suffer with PTSD.

PRIMARY VICTIMS

Primary victims are those who experienced the life-threatening situation first hand. In many instances they are easily identified. The survivors of a major disaster stand a 30-60 per cent risk of developing Post Traumatic Stress Disorder. The risk will vary according to the degree of perceived risk, the duration, and the scale of the event. In many of these cases, people now anticipate a reaction to the trauma. Allowances are made for the victims and it is generally acknowledged that they have experienced an incredible shock. Those involved in a well-publicised tragedy will be overwhelmed by the warmth and compassion of the sympathy expressed towards them.

The novelty wears off after a while. As time passes, those around the victim may be heard to comment that 'It's time she snapped out of it', or 'He should pull himself together and get on with life'. Comments like these show a lack of understanding of PTSD.

Not all primary victims are so obvious. Many life-threatening events go unnoticed by the rest of society. A rape victim may hide her trauma for months, or even years. A victim of incest may always feel unable to disclose the abuse. Victims of bullying are frightened or threatened into keeping quiet. An abused child may simply be labelled hyperactive, or uncontrollable. Many of the children taken into care for their own protection and welfare are actually suffering some of the symptoms of PTSD (Smith 1986). These personal traumatic experiences are the most difficult to talk about, and the most difficult to treat.

SECONDARY VICTIMS

The family and friends of victims often become victims of PTSD themselves. There are two main reasons for this. First, the family may witness scenes from the trauma, either first hand, or by courtesy of the media. For example, many people lost loved ones in the Lockerbie air crash in 1988, where 270 (259 passengers and 11 people on the ground) died. They cannot have avoided seeing the scene on television during the following weeks. Seeing the devastation to the community of Lockerbie and the contorted frame of the nose of the aircraft in an open field could only add to the image of the suffering that might have been endured by a relative or friend. The criminal trial for this bombing was not concluded until 31 January 2001.

Those close to the survivors of a disaster may also suffer in a similar way. In recent years Europe has witnessed two traumatic incidents which involved crowded football stadiums. In May 1985, 56 people died during crowd disturbances at the Heysel Stadium in Belgium. Four years later, overcrowding at the Hillsborough Stadium in England resulted in the deaths of 97 people. The last of these victims lived until 1993 when mechanical life support was suspended. Both incidents involved supporters of Liverpool Football Club, and both events were screened live on television. Relatives and friends watched the live television pictures in horror as people were crushed before their eyes, knowing that somewhere in the crowd was a person they cared for deeply.

Once the survivors returned to the relative safety of their homes, they began to suffer vivid memories of the life-threatening event. Those around them also had mental images of the occasion, and witnessing the primary victim's suffering induced the disorder in secondary victims.

This sequence of events is not limited to disasters that have been broadcast on television. Many relatives witness the trauma first hand if it is a road accident, an assault, or a crime against property such as theft or burglary.

TERTIARY VICTIMS

Tertiary victims are the onlookers or witnesses. They have no link with any person directly involved in the life-threatening event, but they saw what happened. If the event is serious, these victims will probably be called to court or a hearing of some kind to give evidence. Giving evidence is a trauma in itself. The worry of such an ordeal hanging over them for months, sometimes years, means that witnesses are not permitted the luxury of forgetting. Society demands that they keep the memory fresh.

Witnesses, like primary victims, just happen to be there at the time. However, if you are so close to an event that you see it, then before long you are nagged by the thought that 'it could have happened to me'. If it is a road accident then that is not an irrational thought, it is a reality. In consequence, the witnesses may also feel that they have been prey to a life-threatening event. They could have been seriously injured or killed.

THE RESCUERS AND THE CARERS

To a degree, the only victims of PTSD who can prepare themselves to deal with life-threatening events are rescuers and carers. Their job demands that they become involved with primary victims. This involvement is on a deep and personal level for fire, police and ambulance personnel, doctors, nurses, paramedics and counsellors.

Many of these professional people wear a uniform. This may assist at the time. Hiding behind a uniform can be an asset in certain circumstances, but when the uniform is removed, all that remains is another frail human being. True, this is a well-trained, experienced and professional person, but he or she may only face a major disaster once or twice in a working lifetime.

In less traumatic situations, it may be one aspect of the incident which affects professionals in a way that could not have been predicted. In the Lockerbie incident, emergency staff suffered from shock brought about by the meaninglessness of the tragedy. Cases of PTSD were being diagnosed up to two years after the disaster.

The victims of PTSD are many. Those who are not primary victims of the disorder are frequently referred to as hidden victims. For every primary victim of PTSD there could be as many as three hidden victims.

SO WHY ME?

PTSD is selective. Not everyone is affected. Unfortunately, it is not possible to predict who will be affected by this disorder.

There are some indications, however, that particular groups of people may be more susceptible to the disorder than others. People who possess an introverted personality may be at slightly greater risk. A family history of anxiety or depression may be a contributing factor. These ideas are based upon very limited research studies purely because PTSD is such an impossible disorder to monitor.

It appears likely that a person with pre-existing difficulties which create a stressful lifestyle, may have already stretched his or her psychological and emotional defences to near breaking point. The life-threatening trauma will be the final straw.

Carers and rescue workers can have risks reduced by careful training and preparation to expect trauma. Once a traumatic event has been experienced, the personnel involved must be fully, and professionally, counselled in a procedure known as Critical Incident Debriefing (Parkinson 1993).

Nevertheless, a trauma may be so devastating that it affects even the strongest character. It is unreasonable for anyone to suggest that PTSD is self-induced or that if only you could pull yourself together things would be just fine.

In this opening chapter we have looked at trauma, and what Post Traumatic Stress Disorder is. We have also looked at the number of people who suffer with the disorder, and who they might be. Finally, we have established that victims with PTSD are most definitely 'normal' and are not mad. PTSD is a normal emotional reaction to an abnormal, and potentially life-threatening, event.

Before looking at the symptoms and treatments of PTSD, I want to introduce you to a group of people. They are all PTSD victims. They are all real people with feelings and emotions, with families and friends. These are true stories but, quite naturally, the identities have been camouflaged to protect their privacy and confidentiality.

Eleven cases are outlined in the next chapter. These cases reappear throughout the book to explain how these people have combated their PTSD.

The first story is my own.

Chapter two

Personal stories

case	name	age	incident	occupation
			Summary of my case and the 10 other illustrated cases	
1	David	35	physically assaulted	police officer
2	Marlene	43	innocent party in two motoring accidents	nurse
3	Graham	48	brick thrown through his car window	fire officer
4	Cindy	19	hit by falling ladder	student
5	Matthew	25	discovered suicide of friend, then burgled	educationalist
6	Jessica	30	experienced traumatic Caesarean section	shop assistant
7	Richard	41	witnessed house fire, people trapped	police officer
8	Arlette	52	bullied in the workplace	college lecturer
9	Felicity	14	sexually abused by brother	schoolgirl
10	Paul	24	rescued from sinking ship	bank clerk
11	Christine	37	raped by a doctor	architect

CASE 1: DAVID

I was 35 years old when all this happened. I live with my wife and three children in a quiet Oxfordshire village. I had been a police officer for twelve years. Before that I taught geography in a secondary school. The incident occurred on 15 July 1990.

We arrived in Wantage Market Place at 8.45 pm and Tom stopped the car. From this vantage point there was a perfect view of the town centre. Tonight it was not the view we expected. The place was packed with people.

Whatever the event had been, it was now over. A street-cleaning vehicle was clearing rubbish. Judging by the large number of plastic mugs scattered around, a good time had been had by all. The general mood of the crowd was friendly.

A middle-aged male cautiously approached our car. He obviously had a problem.

'I know you two are traffic officers, so you may not be interested ... but there is a fight going on around the other side of the square.'

We spotted the fight. Surrounding the two fighters were about twenty youngsters, jeering and egging them on. We moved in to separate the pair. If we could break up the fight and calm things down, the crowd would soon disperse.

I caught hold of 'Curly', grabbing his arm and steering him away from his opponent. Tom went to the other youth. I did not see Tom again for some considerable time.

The jeering crowd, acting as if directed, split in two: half moving away with Tom, the other half staying with me. I led 'Curly' to the side of our car, still expecting that after a few words he would calm down and listen to reason.

Wrong. His friends tried to pull him away, saying I was picking on him. 'Curly' lashed out, hitting my cheek.

This blow made me revise my assessment of the situation. This was not a problem that could be solved quickly and quietly. The crowd was growing all the time. The pulling and shoving continued but I held on to 'Curly's' arm. I was struck again. The situation was becoming ugly. A tactical withdrawal was required, but I did not want to surrender completely.

'I am arresting you ... ' I started, surprised at my calm voice.

Before I could finish, 'Curly' held up his clenched fists, boxing style, and jeered at me: 'Go on then.'

This seemed to be a golden opportunity. While his fists were raised, I brought my handcuffs out and locked one cuff on his wrist, in one swift movement. My confidence was restored by this successful manoeuvre. Getting the other cuff on was not so easy.

My senses were on red alert by this time. I was surrounded on three sides. My back was to the car. The group pushed forward and I became pinned to the car. Several kicks made contact with the lower half of my body. I tried to push back, and at the same time move 'Curly' to a position between me and the crowd. If they were going to continue kicking, then he could shield me.

There was a rip. Part of my shirt vanished into the crowd. A loud cheer followed.

All I wanted was to get my prisoner into the car, and get out of the square. I twisted the empty half of the handcuffs so that if 'Curly' wanted to keep his arm he would have to follow it. I eventually manoeuvred him between me and the crowd. I was still pinned to the car, so opening its door was impossible.

Then I was knocked to my knees. A kick caught the side of my leg and I went down. When you are on your knees in a crowd you get a different perspective of things. The situation was decidedly unhealthy.

I knew that if I were knocked any lower I would be in serious trouble. As well as being on my knees I had my head pinned against the side of the car. While I was still in this vulnerable position I felt several blows to my body. I was in considerable pain, and felt very frightened.

My left hand was gripping the handcuff. My truncheon was in its long slim pocket running down my right leg. It seemed to take forever to find the strap and work it into a position where I could slide my whole hand through the loop and have a firm grip on the weapon.

I had never used my truncheon before. Out it came, almost unnoticed in the chaos. I had a really firm grip on it, and hit out as hard as I could. Being in a sea of legs, I could not miss. I hit out repeatedly. My attackers retreated enough for me to stand up. I could not see anyone hobbling, but the force of those blows had achieved the desired effect. I was back on my feet and had space to manoeuvre at last. I was still scared.

The radio. All this time I had a personal radio on a strap around my waist. I pulled it up to my mouth and pressed the transmit button.

'Tango Whiskey One Four, urgent assistance required, Wantage Market Place.' I repeated the message. I heard no response, and did not know whether the control room had heard me. Perhaps I simply could not hear the reply because of the noise.

To use the radio I had to let go of the handcuff. I also lost my truncheon. I was hit many times and my memory of exactly what happened next is lost for ever.

I saw a police uniform before me. It was not Tom, so my message must have got through. I looked around. I could count only three other blue uniforms. The odds were still not favourable.

I saw someone inside the patrol car about to smash the radio. I reached in and caught the handset just in time. I pressed the 'transmit' button. The red transmission light came on. Using this set, my message would go straight to force headquarters.

'Tango Whiskey One Four, 10-9 Wantage Market Place.' It was all I had time for. The message was coded, 10-9 meant an officer required immediate assistance.

I could see Tom and four others with their truncheons drawn, in a semicircle, facing outwards. Clearly we still had a fight on our hands. By now there were about 60 youths involved, with many more jeering and shouting.

A police van arrived. After the doors were opened there was a few seconds' delay before a large German Shepherd dog emerged. It was barking and straining on its lead.

The handler let the dog advance. Clearly the animal was eager, but it was also confused. It was facing a group in which it was police officers who were holding weapons - their truncheons. The police dog launched its attack, biting the only police sergeant present at the incident. The handler pulled the dog back and scolded it. The dog sat down, completely confused and no longer inclined to take any further part. The crowd sensed the creature's indecision and charged it. The animal was now as frightened as the rest of us. I had never seen a police dog intimidated in this way before, and realised our position was serious. Were we going to be lynched?

I could not keep going much longer. 'Curly' kneed me in the groin, and someone else banged my head several times on my car. I was having difficulty concentrating. I could feel things slipping sway.

I looked up. There, 100 feet above me was a police helicopter.

I had not heard it at all. To this day I have no recollection of the noise one associates with a helicopter. It was training a searchlight on the group in which I was trapped. I was reassured by its presence, but it spotlighted me as a vulnerable target. It also attracted more people out from the pubs.

At last, some flashing blue lights. There is something very reassuring about the sight and sound of fast, powerful, police patrol cars. Three arrived at the same time, together with the first of four large riot vans each containing 10 officers. The helicopter had at least conveyed the message that we needed help in a big way.

Soon I handed over my prisoner to another officer. The relief at being able to relax my arms was amazing. I looked about me and took stock of the situation. I was aware of chanting:

"Get the pigs"

"Kill the Bill"

The crowd had grown to over 200, with about sixty involved in the fighting. There were now fifty policemen present, and more still arriving.

Someone suggested that Tom and I take our car, with two prisoners, to the police station. I pushed two prisoners into the car; one of them was 'Curly'. Tom got into the driving seat. As I tried to climb into the back of the car with the two prisoners, the crowd surged forward. I was pinned between door and frame.

A woman approached; I supposed that she was related to one to the prisoners. I thought she intended to tell her son precisely what she thought of his behaviour. She came towards me, looked me straight in the eyes, and spat in my face.

As the crowd was forced back by the other officers, I managed to get into the car, stunned by the woman's actions.

The ordeal was not over. The crowd forged forward again and rocked the car.

I briefly recalled a television news clip about an incident in Northern Ireland where a mob attacked a car which contained two soldiers. I remembered how the incident concluded, with both men being murdered, and quickly pushed the thoughts out of my mind.

The sideways movement of the car was sickening. One of the prisoners started to cry. Tom drove the car forward, very slowly. As a gap opened in the crowd he accelerated away to the police station.

CASE 2: MARLENE
Marlene is divorced. She is 43 and lives in Washington State. She served for a time in the armed services but has now settled into a nursing career in a hospital. The incidents she describes occurred in December 1990 and January 1993.

It had been raining for some hours. Many of the roads were flooded with surface water that made driving tricky, sometimes dangerous. I hated driving in this sort of weather although I had never even seen a road accident, let alone been involved in one.

I came towards a junction where the surface water was particularly deep. Cars were crossing on my side of the road in order to go around the water. I slowed right down and came to a gentle halt.

A large truck was coming towards me. The driver clearly did not appreciate how deep the water was and so made no attempt to skirt around the hazard. He drove his vehicle straight through the water, making a bow-wave immediately in front of his own vehicle. As it drew nearer I realised that my little car was in danger of being swamped. I sounded my horn and flashed the car headlamps to try to draw attention my plight.

The truck trundled past, sending a torrent of water cascading over my vehicle. The engine coughed and sputtered in protest at the sudden surge of water, then it cut out altogether. It refused to restart.

Furious, I opened my door and clambered out into the road, and the pouring rain. A horn sounded behind me. I turned to see a car. Moments later it struck me, lifting me high on to the front of the vehicle and carrying me about 20 yards along the road before coming to a stop.

I slid on to the road surface and passed out.

My next memory is of a very wet road, only inches from my eyes. I was in pain everywhere and was soaked to the skin. Looking around as much as I could, I saw several people coming to my assistance - and the car that had hit me was driving off. I passed out again.

Two years later, I was a passenger in a friend's car. We were out on a shopping spree, and looking forward to spending our money. We came to a stop at a road junction and my friend was just about to pull out on to the main road when there was a sickening jolt.

My next recollection is one of a stabbing pain in my neck. My car seat appeared to have vanished. The back of it had collapsed and I was resting at a crazy angle, unable to move. Right beside my window was the front of another car. We had been hit from behind and the impact had caused the other car to spin around so that it was wedged against my door. I could not get out, and the car engine was smoking steadily.

I remember thinking, 'Why me again?' and starting to cry.

Someone was touching my left shoulder gently. I looked around to see a friendly face encouraging me to move across to the other side of the car so as to clamber out. I tried to move but could not get myself off the broken seat.

The face grinned, and produced a large, sharp penknife. He moved forward, bringing the knife up towards my neck. I screamed. Then I almost fell off the seat on to my rescuer. He had cut the seat belt which was preventing me from climbing out of the car. Feeling a complete fool, I managed to follow him across the seats and on to the road. My legs were like jelly, and I hurt everywhere.

Sitting on the grass at the side of the road, someone offered me a blanket which I gratefully accepted. I was now shaking badly. I looked across at the two cars which, inexplicably, were in the middle of the road. My friend's car was a mess. The other car was in flames. I watched in horror as the flames spread like some kind of infection from one vehicle to the other. In no time at all, the spot where I had been sitting became a ball of dancing red and yellow flames.

The shaking grew steadily worse.

CASE 3: GRAHAM

Graham is 48. He lives with his wife in a detached house in rural Cumbria. He was due to retire from the fire service in seven years' time and had already started making plans to emigrate to Australia to join his son's young family. He had worked in the department as a Senior Fire Officer for the past 15 years and was also an experienced driver. The incident occurred in October 1988.

My story is short and simple. It was late one night and I was out in my Fire Officer's car, a white Ford with the word 'FIRE' in big bold letters along the side. I was driving. My young colleague and I were listening to the police band radio. A police vehicle was chasing a stolen motorcycle.

By following the commentary we realised that the stolen vehicle was heading our way. We started to head towards a spot where we might intercept the chase. If there was an accident we may be called upon to cut people free of the wreckage. It was a task we had done before. By anticipating such an incident we could save precious moments if an accident occurred.

We were on the edge of the suburbs, on a fast route which bypassed the city centre. Many minor roads passed over the route on specially constructed over-bridges. As was often the case, groups of young people were gathering on some of these bridges to watch the traffic go by. With little other local entertainment, this was a normal occurrence, but one which was generally discouraged by the local police.

The stolen motorcycle was only about two miles away and we were rapidly closing the gap between us. The fire car was fitted with blue flashing lights which were now switched on to warn other motorists as we sped along the road in the outside lane at about 80 mph. There was very little traffic on this section of the road, and we were making good progress. Our car was capable of 120 mph, and I gently started to increase its speed.

I had been involved in incidents like this hundreds of times before. Even so, I still felt alert and keen to be of assistance if required.

We were about 500 yards from one of the over-bridges, and I was aware if a small group of youngsters standing on the bridge above our lane of traffic. The street lights were not particularly good, but I could see a few of the youngsters jumping up and down, waving their arms about. I suspected they had been drinking. The chill in the air would soon drive them all home, I hoped.

Then I saw the brick. One youth was holding it high above his head. He was going to throw it at our car. I thought the chance of him timing his throw exactly right was only slim, but I didn't particularly want a brick to smash through our windscreen whilst we were travelling at ... almost 90 mph now. My concentration became divided between driving and watching the youth with the brick.

Everything shifted into a kind of slow motion. The distance between our car and the bridge decreased steadily. The youth's arms windmilled forward and I saw the brick launch into the air. I was unable to take my eyes off it. My right foot moved from the accelerator pedal to the brake pedal, but it took an age to leave one and find the other. I pushed down on the brake, but the car seemed very slow to respond to the pressure.

My colleague shouted a warning, but that too was in slow motion. My arms moved the steering wheel to the left so as to move from the path of the brick as it dropped towards us. It only measured nine inches by four inches, but it looked so big now.

Suddenly the windscreen shattered and I felt a stabbing pain in my head and shoulder. The car hit one of the bridge supports and came to a halt on the grass beside the road and I sank back into the driving seat. There was a big hole in the windscreen, just to my side of the centre. I could see my colleague using the radio but I was unable to hear what he was saying. I don't even remember hearing the windscreen smash.

There was a lot of blood around. We were both bleeding from cuts on our faces and I could not move my left shoulder. We appeared to sit on our own, in silence, for an age before friendly *faces started to appear. First to arrive was a police car, then an ambulance. I remember thinking that someone was going to have to cut me free from all this, then I mentally switched off and cannot remember much more.*

CASE 4: CINDY

Cindy is 19 years old. She is single and lives with her parents in a semi-detached house on the edge of a town in Norfolk. Having dropped out of school, she is now trying to make up for her lack of qualifications by training as a computer programmer. Prior to the incident in June 1990, Cindy had an extrovert nature.

I was heavily into punk rock. I had the crazy Mohican hairstyle, coloured blue and red. I wore studs in both ears and in my nose. My clothes identified me as an individual with very bad taste. I liked loud music and even louder friends.

Each day, after college, I would walk along the High Street towards the bus station where I had to wait at least 30 minutes for my bus to take me out of town to where I lived with my parents. I often walked along the street with my personal stereo blasting my ears into my kind of heaven. I was oblivious to the rest of the world. On the day of the accident, I left college a little late. Even so, I knew I had plenty of time to walk to the bus station. The stereo was on full power. The people around me could probably hear the music too.

One of the main stores in the High Street was being renovated. Scaffolding had been erected around the structure and numerous posters apologised for any inconvenience that these alterations may cause. The promised completion date had already passed and there was no sign that the work was nearly finished except for the increased number of goods vehicles making deliveries that day.

I had lost interest in the building work long ago. I simply saw it as another obstacle which hindered my progress towards the bus station. The footpath was narrowed by the building work and, in consequence, people were forced to walk that much more closely together than they would normally. It felt as if my own personal space was being invaded by strangers. I didn't like it, but no way was I going to show that it concerned me. I wore an air of indifference as I dodged and weaved my way through the crowd.

I expect that, had I not been wearing the stereo, I would have heard some warning - some audible clue that things were about to go horribly wrong. I was in my own little world though - Miss Independent, that's me.

Suddenly the people around me moved away. The crowd thinned and I could actually see where I was putting my feet. I realise now that some people tried to warn me, but I simply ignored everyone. What I could not ignore was the 30-foot-long steel ladder which landed right on top of me. I fell in a crumpled heap.

I came to, on the concrete, with blood oozing from a wound to my head. There were all sorts of noises going on inside my head, than I realised that the stereo was still playing, I tried to move my hands to remove the earphones but my arms wouldn't work properly. I was aware of something heavy resting on top of me.

Suddenly it all went quiet. I thought I was dead. It must all go quiet when you die. I could feel someone touching my head. It hurt and I wanted them to stop. I tried to speak but couldn't. I was not dead, but it felt like I was dying.

'It's not fair, I'm still a virgin,' I thought to myself. I tried to move again. This time I had a little more success. My arm came up against something cold, something metallic. I tried to look at what I had touched and saw that part of a ladder was only inches from my face. I could not move because the ladder was across my body. I closed my eyes and wished someone would move the ladder for me. Then someone tried to move the ladder and it hurt my head. I wished they would leave it alone until I felt a little better. I remembered that it was considered bad luck to walk under a ladder. Now I knew why.

At that point I must have lost consciousness.

CASE 5: MATTHEW

Matthew is 25, single and a keen sportsman. He works for the education service of a coastal town in California. He has his own modest house and an active social life. The two events he describes occurred in March 1991 and November 1991.

It was all so unexpected. I wanted to call around and see my friend to discuss the fishing trip we were going to make together at the weekend. I was really looking forward to the peace and quiet of the lake, a few beers, and a good long chat about anything and everything.

There was no answer at the front door, but I could hear the dog barking inside. I had tried ringing a few minutes earlier, but the telephone was engaged. John was in, so why didn't he answer the door?

I went around to the back of the house, and rapped on the door there. The dog still barked, but I didn't hear the approaching footsteps which would have heralded John's arrival at the door. Looking through the window I could see the dog. However, the dog was not looking my way, it was looking into the living room and continuing to bark.

I didn't really like dogs much and had no great understanding of their habits. (I'm not really keen on any animals.) I did know, though, that when you knocked on a door, the dog barked at the door and not into the room away from the door. Something was wrong. Perhaps John was ill. I had to find a way of getting into the house to check that everything was OK.

I started to hunt around for an open window. Nothing. I tried my own keys in the locks without any real expectation that they would work. I was not surprised. I was going to have to break in. I knocked on the door again. The dog continued to bark. The noise was starting to get on my nerves.

Picking up a large stone I smashed it against one of the small panes of glass in the back door. It made a terrible noise and I half expected neighbours to start flooding out of their homes, accusing me of burglary. Reaching inside the smashed window I hunted for the key that should be in the lock on the inside of the door. Finding it at last I unlocked the door, withdrew my hand and tried to open the door. It wouldn't budge.

I remembered that there was a bolt at the top of the door. Smashing another piece of glass I managed to slide back the bolt and the door opened when I tried it for the second time.

Standing in the doorway I waited for the dog to bound up to me. I wished I could remember the creature's name. But he did not come bounding up to me. This made me nervous and, looking around the kitchen, I selected a large sharp knife and, thus armed, I moved cautiously towards the living room.

I don't know what I expected to find exactly, but what I did find took me by surprise. John was sitting in his armchair by the fireplace. On the floor beside his chair was a glass and an empty bottle of scotch. His lap was covered in a deep reddish-brown stain. John had cut both his wrists, and had probably done so some hours ago. He was dead.

I rushed to the telephone - not that the situation required urgency, but it seemed appropriate at the time. I stopped and stared at the instrument. It was one of those cordless devices that you could take with you as you wander around the house. The handset was missing and two little red lights on the base set were illuminated. I started to hunt for the handset. No wonder I could not get through to John on the phone.

I found the handset on the floor alongside the empty glass by John's chair. As I reached down to pick it up, I realised that I was still holding the kitchen knife I had so bravely armed myself with earlier. Picturing how John had died, I dropped the knife in horror. Slowly backing out of the room, I turned, and rushed out of the back door. I had to find a neighbour and use her phone. I was not looking forward to the next few hours.

It had been some months since John's funeral. My life had returned to normal, although I greatly missed my friend. Returning home from work one day, I noticed that the door to my flat was wide open. Somebody was inside. I walked quietly into the hallway and through to the kitchen. I could hear the noise of cupboards and drawers being opened in the dining room. Somebody was going through my things. Without really thinking, I opened a drawer and took out a kitchen knife to arm myself.

'He might have a gun. The sensible thing to do would be to run,' I told myself. I ignored my own advice. Throwing caution to the wind, I rushed to the dining room door and flung it wide open. A young man looked up from the cupboard he was searching and saw me standing there with the knife raised. A look of panic crossed his face and his eyes darted around the room looking for an escape route.

Suddenly, my mind took me back to John's house and the way I had walked into his living room with a knife raised in the expectation that John was being burgled. Then I could see John sitting in my chair, wrists cut, bleeding all over the floor. I backed into the hall and started to shake violently.

My young burglar couldn't believe his luck. Pushing me backwards, he rushed past me and out of the door. It was some considerable time before I managed to get back on to my feet and close the outside door. What had happened to me?

CASE 6: JESSICA

Jessica was 30 at the time of this event. She is married and has one daughter. She works part-time in a local grocery store in southern Pennsylvania where she now lives. Jessica suffered for many years before her condition was recognised as PTSD. The incident took place in January 1981.

I was nine months pregnant and feeling on top of the world until that morning when I realised the time had come for me to give birth. I had enjoyed the pregnancy, survived the morning sickness and revelled in the attention I received from my family and friends. It had previously been agreed that the best way for the baby to be born was by Caesarean section, so off to the hospital I went.

I was well prepared. My bag had been packed for several weeks, new nightdresses and toiletries had been purchased well in advance. I was booked into the hospital ward and introduced to some of the nursing staff. They were all warm and welcoming. It was my first baby but I assured myself that these people had done it all many times before and that I was in safe hands.

It came to the time when I was taken from the ward, along endless corridors to the operating suite. I felt rather vulnerable stretched out on the trolley bed. All I was able to do was watch the ceiling as I was moved from one area to another. I noticed cracks and peeling paint, all manner of uninteresting things. The longer the journey lasted the more anxious I became. Eventually, I arrived at the entrance to the operating suite.

I was left alone. Looking about me, I saw that I had a clear view into the operating theatre. The door was wide open. I was being watched constantly by the anaesthetist. I could see all the staff in masks, green clothes and green boots on their feet. I was terrified. The room in which they stood looked sterile and cold. It was full of equipment, shiny surfaces and bright lights.

I was on a trolley, or gurney, but suddenly someone put the sides up like metal bars on the side of a cot. There was no warning of what was happening. Nobody spoke to me. I suddenly felt very lonely. Oh, I felt so closed in by the bars and there appeared to be no escaping my fate.

I was left like this for nearly 30 minutes because the obstetrician who was going to perform the operation had not yet arrived. During that time, I could see them all walking in and out and looking down at me. I started to think seriously about all the things that could go wrong. I desperately wanted a reassuring voice to talk to. Someone to hold my hand perhaps, and tell me it would be all right. By the end of the 30 minutes I was convinced that I was going to die in that operating theatre. All around me there were voices talking in hushed, giggling tones about me. I wanted to jump off the trolley and run, run anywhere. It seems impossible, but I had forgotten about the baby, my husband, everything. All I could think of was escaping the operating theatre and almost certain death. That's the last thing I remember.

When I came round after the operation I was a different person. My baby was safe and well, but I was nervous wreck. I was jumpy. The slightest noise startled me. I found myself constantly studying the rest of the ward, on the watch for any possible dangers. It was crazy. What possible danger could I be in, in a hospital ward?

I dreaded the doctors or nurses pulling the curtains around my bed. It felt so claustrophobic. I started having nightmares about doctors with knives in their hands walking towards me. It was terrifying, and in the time I stayed in hospital I developed a fear of moving outside the ward. I just could not, and did not want to go out.

When I was home it got worse. I ignored the doorbell. I used to run past the telephone in the house. I was actually frightened of the object. When it rang I was petrified. I never answered it, *my feet and legs turned to jelly, I felt sick in my stomach. I had panic attacks. I just couldn't understand what had happened to me.*

CASE 7: RICHARD

Aged 41, Richard works as a police officer in an inner city area in Mississippi State. He has three teenage children by his first marriage and had married again in 1987. He has been a police officer for 20 years and has 'seen it all'. This traumatic event occurred in August 1992.

The house was a large terraced property. The basement had grilles over the front and back windows and the door had several locks - safety precautions which are not unusual for the area.

The family of five lived in the basement. There was a history of domestic fights, and recently they had become quite vicious. While the family slept, the door was made secure and the keys thrown from the window. The children woke to find petrol being poured on them by their father. The basement flat was set alight. A web of fire quickly spread all around the mother and her children. There was no way out of the flat. They smashed the grille-covered windows to get air, and to yell for help.

A family above heard the commotion and raised the alarm. They made an abortive attempt to try to smash the door down, but were beaten by its strength. I was in a passing police car which was flagged down at the end of the block. There was not time to prepare myself, mentally and physically, for what was about to happen in the next few minutes.

Stopping outside the front of the house, I saw the smoke coming from the basement windows. I saw, and heard, the victims as they stood as close to the fresh air as they could get. Red flames flickered behind them. I thought it was a picture of hell with arms waving hopelessly and cries for help.

It became obvious that the door was not going to give way. The people who had been putting their shoulders to it were now getting tired, and were also being affected by the thickening smoke. The area in front of the door was restricted by stairs and rubbish bins. There was not much room in which to work. I ran down the stairway to take over at the door. It appeared hopeless, but I had at least to try. I passed the window and recoiled in horror as arms reached out to try and grab me. I felt sick deep down inside.

I got a lung full of smoke and that frightened me as I gasped for breath. Looking round, I saw that I was alone at the door. The other people had retreated back up the stairway to the street.

I wanted to leave, but couldn't. I couldn't leave those people to die without hope. I could still see them watching me from the window. I tried the door again, but it held firm. I accepted that I was going to have to watch them die. There was nothing more I could do.

I saw the mother holding a young boy up to the window trying to give him some air, and to protect him from the fire. The fire was smouldering as there was clearly not a lot of air in the basement. The flames seemed to be like some dark animal in the background. It appeared inevitable that the flames were going to slowly advance towards the window and consume the helpless figures who stood there.

I was unable to speak to them, I felt so helpless. I looked away and swallowed hard. I remembered hearing that it was possible to force a door if you sat on the floor and braced yourself against the opposite wall. My legs were like jelly, but it was worth one last effort before the smoke became too thick.

I decided that I would stay by the door, trying to force it open, until the people inside lost consciousness and disappeared from the window. I did not want them to witness me giving up. I accepted that I might be injured myself, but that those injuries would be slight compared with the suffering inside the basement.

The door gave slightly at the bottom, but then sprang back into place. The whole incident was taking on an air of unreality. Then suddenly the door gave way and opened. I shouted for others to help me. I was unsure what to do next. Should I go inside?

The children came to the front door, followed by their mother. Now that the door was open, air was rushing into the building and the fire intensified. Flames were now licking around the windows. I told everyone to crouch low, cover their mouths and run up the stairway.

Looking inside the door, I could see a room and a male body on the floor. He was badly burned. I charged inside and grabbed hold of him, but he made no effort to move himself. I managed to drag him towards the door and screamed for others to come and help me. I was scared. The fire was burning fiercely now, the far wall of the room where I stood was like a red waterfall. Another policeman joined me and we half carried, half dragged the person out of the basement. At one point the body fell across the doorway, blocking my exit from the basement. This caused me to panic and scream at him to get up and move. I swore at him repeatedly as I tried to move him outside. At one point I even kicked at him to make him move.

My memory has blanked out some of this struggle, but we managed to get everyone to the top of the stairway where others took over from me. Eventually the fire trucks arrived at the building. By this time the flames were reaching the footpath. The injured were stretched out in the street; there was nowhere for them to go until an ambulance arrived.

I started to feel very weak and sank to the ground. I was unable to act or think clearly any more. I just watched as others ran around me dealing with the injured and the fire. Eventually I was taken to hospital, suffering from 'shock'. There I learned that the man I had half dragged from the basement had died. It was also alleged that he had caused the fire in the first place.

I shed no tears for him.

CASE 8: ARLETTE

At the age of 52, I considered myself to be reaching the peak of my career as a lecturer in a teacher's training college situated in the north of England. However, I soon realised that some of my colleagues saw me as a challenge, a threat. In a short time my life was turned upside-down. I became a physical and mental wreck. Why? Because those around me were bullying me. It began when the college was going through a period of reorganisation. As part of this restructuring they awarded my job to a junior member of my staff. My newly promoted "junior" became the ringleader in a reign of tactical psychological abuse.

Whatever the outcome of the meeting, I knew I was going to be out of a job before many more weeks had passed. I had been refused eye contact by my colleagues. Their body language was extremely negative toward me. At departmental meetings I was not allowed to speak, and they later treated anything I did offer as without value. Brochures about retraining courses were left anonymously in my staff pigeonhole. They orchestrated everything to make me feel totally unwanted.

My new manager had phoned on Friday evening to inform me of a meeting that I must attend on the following Tuesday. My attendance was demanded. The content of the meeting was described as "too important to divulge in advance." It was all engineered so that I endured a sleepless weekend. My partner was aware that something was wrong but I just shrugged it off as 'stress' at work.

The time of the meeting eventually arrived. I was asked a question. I started to answer only to be interrupted with a second question. When I tried to answer the second question I was accused of evading the first and was then asked a third, unconnected, question. This went on and on. In a nutshell, they told me that my opinions were known, I was a troublemaker. To deny this bizarre allegation simply proved I was a liar too! I was told that my "boyfriend" was a bad influence. The term "boyfriend" was uttered in a way that inferred that the relationship was disgusting. I wanted to fight back but I was so distressed and confused I did not know where to begin. I left in tears.

People started to refuse to work with me. Every conceivable tactic of psychological abuse, short of physical torture, was used. Life was hell.

Whenever I saw my new manager on the campus I was spoken of loudly and rudely to anyone he was with. My colleagues mocked me and either derided or hid any evidence of my successes. An unsolicited letter of praise from a teacher who was acting as mentor to one of my students on teaching practice was openly laughed at by those to whom it was shown. I was labelled a troublemaker by more senior managers when I complained of this victimisation.

Eventually there came the day when they wanted to dismiss me from my post. The day they that suspended me I suffered a complete breakdown. I was unable to speak during the hearing. It was all so one-sided. Afterwards, when the principal approached me, I started to cry. The principal said that I should not worry about him (the principal) because he had been through these procedures before. He actually thought that the tears were for him!

The final dismissal proceedings were a fiasco. I was very ill and just wanted to get out. Others saw this as my acceptance that I was wrong in some way. I was ill for over a year. As a way to try to understand the experience I set out to study the subject of adult bullying. Little is written about the subject. So, I wrote to a national publication and my story was widely reported in the press, radio and television.

I now understand that for most people it is easier to sack victims rather than perpetrators. People think twice before openly victimising a black person, or making offensive sexist remarks. Employers do not tolerate these practices because the courts can award huge financial damages in such cases. Similar abuse, disguised as bullying in the workplace, attracts very little attention and generally goes unpunished. I found the vindictive attitude of so many of my colleagues incredible. However, I know there are many others just like me.

CASE 9: FELICITY

Felicity was just 14 years old when all this started. At that time, she lived at home with her parents and older brother. She worked well at school and her future looked promising. She loved the quiet Cheshire village in which she lived. Her father had once been prosecuted for drinking and driving. Felicity never forgot the embarrassment of the court case. These events took place between March 1990 and November 1991.

It all started one night when I had a bad dream, I was being arrested for something I didn't do and was putting up a pretty good fight. I awoke from the dream to find myself sitting upright in bed and being cuddled by my older brother. He was stroking the back of my head and talking to me in a smooth calm voice.

I pulled back from him a little, then relaxed as I realised what had happened. I must have been calling out in my sleep and, as

Mum and Dad were away, Michael had come into my room to see what was the matter.

I relaxed and laid back down on my pillows. Michael smiled and tidied my bed covers. He was 18, nearly five years older than me. We got on well together, however. We seemed to understand each other. He blew me a kiss goodnight and left the room.

Three nights later, I woke again to feel somebody beside me. I did not remember having any dream but guessed I must have done. I had been troubled by the same dream (being arrested) quite a bit recently. Michael was with me again. He was stroking my arm and talking quietly to me. It felt nice and I wasn't worried in the least. Then he pulled back the covers and slid into bed beside me. I rested my arm across him and drifted back to sleep. When I woke in the morning I was on my own.

The pattern continued for some weeks.

One night in July it was really hot. I could not stand my nightdress sticking to me, so I slept on top of the covers, naked. The sound of the door closing woke me and I saw Michael walk quietly towards my bed. I knew I had not woken him so wondered what the matter was. He stood beside my bed, looking at me and I could just make out his smile. His hand reached down and touched my breast. I turned away and tried to find my quilt to cover me up.

Michael sat on the bed and started to touch me again. I tried to sit up but he pushed me back, quite gently, and put his finger to his lips. I didn't like what he was doing.

Michael stayed with me for some time that night. He hurt me and I felt dirty. In the morning I showered, changed the bedclothes and placed all the dirty laundry in the washing machine before breakfast. I think my parents thought I had wet the bed, but nothing was said. I could not look at Michael when he came down to breakfast. In comparison, he was laughing and fooling around in his usual way as if nothing had happened.

Michael came to my room quite often after that. I hated him for it, but felt that I was powerless to stop it. I couldn't tell anyone - Michael told me what he would do to me if I ever told. My parents would only argue, and it might be my fault! I started sleeping with my clothes on.

About 18 months later, I was with a group of friends after school. One of them had managed to get hold of some 'stuff' and we had agreed to meet and share it. There were about six of us in a little group when someone shouted 'Police'. I saw the car and started to run. There were only two officers but both appeared to run after me. It wasn't long before one of them caught hold of my arm and pulled me to a stop. I kicked out at her and tried to scratch. I felt I was fighting for my life.

It was all so much like my dream. The arrest that I had been dreading was now taking place. It was the first time I had been involved with any kind of drugs, and I had been caught. I also had a strange feeling that the woman officer knew all about me and Michael. I was frightened. What were they going to do with me?

CASE 10: PAUL

Paul is 24 and single. He lives in a flat on his own; his last relationship ended when the girl moved out. He works for a European Bank and frequently travels between England and the Continent. The event which nearly cost him his life took place in March 1987.

It was March 1987 and I had enjoyed my first trip of the year to the Continent. Everything was as it should be. I was in a great mood and looking forward to the crossing.

It was all so sudden. One minute I was sitting quietly by the window on the right hand side of the ship. I couldn't see much outside because of the way the light caught the glass. There was no hint of trouble. People were all around, talking in excited voices. Smiles and happy faces, that's what I remember.

Then there was a shudder and the ship started to move over to the left. I was rising higher and the people to my left were being lowered. It was an awful sensation. I lost my bearings and could not work out what was happening. Then the lights went out. I tumbled out of my seat and fell. I fell for what appeared to be for ever. Then I landed with a thump which knocked all the air out of my body. I didn't move for quite a while. I just lay still, trying to work out exactly what was going on. Was it all some kind of dream, a nightmare?

Something moved underneath me. I was on top of somebody. In fact, I was on top of several people. Someone screamed. That started several others. The air filled with screams and shouts. I was travelling on my own, so had nobody to shout to. That didn't stop me calling out for help.

Above the noise of the shouting were all sorts of other strange noises. Creaks and groans that I could not identify. Then I realised what it was. The ship must have struck something, or run aground, and we were sinking. The ship had turned on to its side, throwing me from my seat, and we were going to sink.

I panicked. What could we do? What could I do? Were we going to die? Would anyone rescue us? I recalled films of sea disasters and reminded myself to stay calm. If the ship turned over, there would still be air inside it and we would be rescued by somebody. That's what happened in the films. But in the films, sometimes the passengers died. The panic intensified.

I started to climb up. I could not see much, but my eyes were slowly getting used to the gloom. I climbed on to the edge of a seat, and then on to the seat above that. The ship was at an angle of about 60 degrees and the angle was growing steadily steeper. Climbing up the seats was becoming more and more difficult.

Others started to climb, too. Some complained of pains in arms, legs and chests. Clearly there had already been some injuries, maybe even some deaths. I started to feel guilty about the person I had fallen upon. He had not spoken or moved. Perhaps I had knocked him unconscious when I landed so heavily upon him.

The voices quietened, people started to breathe more heavily as they clambered over the ship's furniture. A few called out to their family. Some sobbed to themselves. It just didn't feel real.

The ship shuddered again suddenly. One or two people fell again. There was a scream to one side of me. Water was coming into the cabin. I could hear it clearly. I started to climb again. I had to get as far away from the water as I could. I think I was close to an exit when someone pulled me backwards and pushed past me. I fell to the floor once again.

I have no real memory of what happened next. I somehow found myself sitting in a helicopter. I was soaked to the skin and had what turned out to be a badly broken arm. Sitting beside me was a woman with a nasty cut on her forehead. We were both shivering despite the warm blankets we had been given. I couldn't believe that I was safe. I later learned that 192 people had died in the ship or in the sea nearby.

CASE 11: CHRISTINE

Christine is 37 years old, married with two daughters. She lives with her family in a smart detached house on the south Devonshire coast. She works as an architect for a large partnership, and has just been made a junior partner in the firm. She has a company car, and is developing a successful career. The event she describes took place in September 1991.

This is not an easy story for me to tell. I considered myself to be a modern liberated woman. Not a feminist, not sexist, but good at my job, and usually able to handle most people and most situations which presented themselves. Consequently, this experience has wrecked my self-confidence, and my control over my life.

It was late in the day, and I had just one more call to make. I was visiting a doctor's surgery. One of the doctors was opening a new practice and I was designing the premises for him. I had built up a good working relationship with the doctors and had already attended several meetings at the old surgery. This last visit had been rearranged, but I saw nothing unusual in that I was expected to call at the surgery outside normal hours. Many doctors preferred to see 'non-patients' at that time of the day. This fitted in with their pattern of house calls and other commitments.

The front door to the surgery was unlocked and I could see a few lights on. The early evening sun was starting to fade and I felt slightly chilly in just my skirt and blouse. Once inside the building, it was easy to follow the signs to the doctor's consulting room. I made a mental note to discuss signing for the new building. The door was ajar but from force of habit, I swapped my briefcase to my left hand and tapped on the door with my right.

The door opened abruptly and a smiling face appeared. Initially, I took a brief step back. The suddenness had momentarily startled me. However, I quickly regained my composure and returned the smile. Introductions were unnecessary as we had met on at least six previous occasions.

'Come in, come in, take your clothes off!'

'Pardon?'

'Sorry. Little joke there. I'm off on holiday tomorrow, so I'm feeling a little light-hearted and happy just now. Would you like a drink?'

'A coffee would be wonderful, thank you.'

'I was thinking of something with a little more life in it.'

'In that case, I think I'll take a rain check on that. I have to drive home later.'

I should have realised at this point that it was not going to be a standard meeting, but I guessed that a doctor about to go off on holiday was entitled to feel a little relief at the prospect and, in consequence, be a little less official/formal than I would usually expect.

Sitting down, I noticed that I was being given the 'once-over'. His gaze was definitely somewhere between hip and knee. I recrossed my legs, smoothing my skirt tidily to just above my knees, and tried to put any silly thoughts out of my mind. This man was a doctor after all.

I opened my briefcase and pulled out a bundle of papers I didn't really need, but I felt more confident with them in my hand. I asked if he had the financial calculations ready for me.

'All in good time, all in good time.' There was that smile again. He pulled his chair a little closer and rubbed his hands together. Then he placed one on my knee. Inside I shuddered, but managed to smile and gently remove his hand while I uncrossed and recrossed my legs. I turned my body slightly towards the door.

'Actually, I'm a little pushed for time, so if you don't have the figures ready, perhaps I could call back for them some other time?'

'No. No, they are here. I'll just have to find them for you, Christine.'

He stood and wandered over to the filing cabinet by the door. I started to return the papers to my briefcase but the door slamming shut made me jump and some of the papers spilled on to the floor. Looking up, I saw him standing in front of the now closed door, still with that awful smile - sort of menacing.

'Let's stop mucking about, shall we? You agreed to come here at this time. What did you expect?'

My skin started to crawl. The hairs at the back of my neck tingled. The penny had dropped. What a fool I had been. In a rush, I jammed the rest of the papers into my briefcase and stood up. I had to leave as quickly as possible. This had gone far enough.

I tried to dodge around the outstretched arms but couldn't avoid them in the confines of the room. He pulled me towards him and tried to kiss me. Turning away, I started to call out but his hand clamped over my mouth and he pushed me backwards. The smile had vanished. His face was shiny with perspiration. His eyes had a cold look about them. His free hand started to roam over my body.

I don't know where I got the strength from, but my knee came up and he jumped backwards to avoid it. I broke free, only to feel a sharp pain in my stomach as a punch took all my breath away.

'That's the way it's going to be, is it, Christine?'

'Let me go now, and that will be the end of it.'

'Oh no.' He moved forward again. 'I'm going to have you, Christine. You know you want it, too. Either way, though, I'm stronger that you, and the building is empty. Nobody will hear.'

He moved forward and grabbed me again. The full realisation of his words made me turn cold. There was little I could do. I had never felt so helpless in my life. I looked around for a weapon, but the room was too tidy. There was nothing for me to use.

I could feel the wall behind me. My back was pressed against it as he came forward again. In one sudden lunge he was pressed against me, his mouth searching for mine as I struggled to pull away. I could feel his hands on me, freeing my clothing. I felt angry, sick, disgusted and cross with myself, although I still could not understand how I could possibly have given all the signals which had led to this situation developing.

It was almost 20 minutes before I could escape from that room. I must have looked a complete wreck as I ran from the building to the side street where I had parked my car. Locking myself in the vehicle I closed my eyes and tried to block out the memory of what had happened. But even with my eyes tightly shut I could still see that awful grin.

How could I possibly tell anyone what had happened to me?

Chapter three

Symptoms of PTSD

Part of the counselling process is to look at what symptoms are being suffered and to explain the messages that the body and mind are sending. Symptoms of PTSD fall into three broad groups: intrusive, avoidant and physical. Taken individually, some symptoms may appear to be minor irritations with no cause for concern. Taken in any combination, these same symptoms can destroy a person's lifestyle, friendships, employment prospects and relationships at home. Self-esteem just evaporates.

Untreated these symptoms can last a lifetime. It is therefore vital that the reactions are seen for what they are: the natural consequence of being confronted with a traumatic, life-threatening event. The four types of symptom are linked closely to the diagnostic table describing PTSD which is cited earlier in the book and repeated here:

Simplification of the six criteria which need to be met before a diagnosis of Post Traumatic Stress Disorder can be made (DSM-IV) (Kinchin 1998)

1. TRAUMA	The person must be exposed to a traumatic event or events that involve actual or threatened death or serious injury, or threat to the physical integrity of self or others. The person's response must involve fear, helplessness or horror.
2. INTRUSIVE	The event must be persistently relived by the person.
3. AVOIDANT	The person must persistently avoid stimuli associated with the trauma.
4. PHYSICAL	The person must experience persistent symptoms of increased arousal, or 'over-awareness'.

5. SOCIAL   The disturbance must cause significant distress or impairment in social, occupational, or other areas of functioning important to the person.

6. TIME   Symptoms, linked to 2, 3 and 4 above, must have lasted at least a month.

Not everyone who experiences the first five criteria will be troubled by the symptoms for over a month. It is only those who continue to suffer after that period who can be confirmed as suffering from Post Traumatic Stress Disorder.

If the disorder is successfully treated within three months, it is described as an acute case of PTSD. Over half of those initially affected have recovered three months later and can therefore be defined as acute PTSD survivors.

When the condition persists for more than three months, a person is described as suffering chronic PTSD. In these instances, the 'trauma beliefs' have become less susceptible to influence, repeated avoidance behaviour is well established, and survivors are far more likely to default from counselling. Consequently, the chronic condition is often compounded by feelings of depression and anxiety, and treatment or support becomes more difficult.

When a person encounters a traumatic, life-threatening event, the brain juggles between recalling the painfulness of the event (intrusions) and going to great lengths to forget it (avoidance). The sufferer's mood will seesaw between the two. Each process has its own set of symptoms which, in turn, act as a catalyst for the physical symptoms to develop.

There are many symptoms of Post Traumatic Stress Disorder. Not all are experienced by every survivor.

INTRUSIVE
    Recurrent and distressing recollections
    Flashbacks, thoughts, nightmares, dreams
    Phobias about specific daily routines, events or objects
    Feelings of guilt for having survived

AVOIDANT
    Detachment from others, emotional numbness
    Avoidance of thoughts or feelings associated with the event
    Markedly diminished interest or pleasure in most activities

PHYSICAL
  Sleep problems
  Hypervigilance
  Exaggerated startle response
  Joint/muscle pains
  Feelings of nervousness
SOCIAL
  Violent outbursts
  Increased irritability
  Impaired memory
  Inability to concentrate
  Irrational or impulsive behaviour
  Low self-esteem
TIME
  Depression/anxiety

Following a traumatic incident, those exposed to the trauma will start to exhibit a number of symptoms (Hamblen 1998). The symptoms will not all present themselves together - some will not appear at all. But during the weeks and months of the aftermath of a traumatic incident some symptoms may occur. They are detailed below. Each symptom is like a small time bomb - circumstances or events may trigger the explosion.

Recurrent and intrusive distressing recollections of the event
It is perhaps obvious, but important, to stress that the recollections of the traumatic event must be intrusive; they must be distressing, and they must be recurrent. It is not just a case of remembering what happened and becoming sad or upset by the memory. For example, a person who is quietly sitting and working on a crossword puzzle may pause from the task in hand, and experience a distressing memory of the car accident he witnessed a few weeks ago.

Subsequently the same person may have thoughts about the accident and start to feel guilty that it was not him that called for the ambulance - he simply stood and stared not knowing what to do for the best. These recollections intrude into the survivor's memory and regularly cause distress and associated strong emotional feelings.

Recurrent and distressing dreams of the event

These dreams, like the recollections, must be recurrent and they must cause distress. However, most people experience the occasional nightmare. A person who dreams of falling of a cliff and awakes in a cold sweat has simply had a bad dream. To qualify as a symptom of PTSD dreams should occur frequently and they should be linked directly to the trauma that has been suffered. The dreams may feature the whole traumatic event, or they might single out one or two aspects of the trauma which were particularly frightening.

Suddenly acting or feeling as if the event were recurring (flashbacks)

The sudden acting out of the traumatic event as though it were happening all over again is usually referred to as a flashback. Flashbacks are extremely frightening for those who experience them and for those who witness the flashback.

The trauma victim may describe the flashback experience as 'having a video camera in their head'. The camera has a video tape of the trauma which suddenly starts running and the trauma is relived just as if it were happening all over again. For the survivor the problem centres on the fact they have no control over the play button on the video camera. The tape suddenly starts running and the survivor is thrown back into the trauma and it is all very real once again.

Furthermore, during a flashback the survivor loses the ability to distinguish between the past and the present as events merge into a single horrific trauma. Victims behave as though they are experiencing the original traumatic event and may be unaware of their behaviour and people around them. When the flashback subsides they will need a period of time to readjust to where they are. They will probably feel frightened and embarrassed and may even entertain the thought they may be "going mad". They will need sympathy and reassurance.

Jessica:
I was out shopping and I suddenly felt that the shop was very crowded. I froze. I could see myself waiting to go into the operating theatre. I was looking down on myself. It was all so real. I couldn't get the picture out of my mind. I could almost

reach out and touch myself. It was over as suddenly as it started. I then felt very foolish and imagined everyone in the store to be looking at me. I had to abandon my shopping and leave.

N.B. A recurrence of the trauma in the form of a flashback is far more involved than a straightforward recollection of the event although both will be distressing.

Intense psychological distress at exposure to cues of the event, phobias

Traumatised people may develop fears and phobias about everyday objects and situations. They have quickly learned that particular sights, sounds, smells or situations will remind them of the trauma they experienced. This knowledge creates a sense of fear, anxiety, anger or impending doom when they come into contact with the cue which might trigger a reminder of the event.

A soldier who witnessed a shooting may suddenly become frightened when he hears a car backfire or a door slam shut. This fright might make him disinclined to go outside where he might be subjected to sudden noises and a form of agoraphobia may develop. A child who was abused whilst camping might develop a quite irrational fear of the sight of camping gas cylinders, or caravans, both being reminders of the location where she was abused.

Being unable to face certain situations or continue with the ordinary course of daily activities because of the possibility of reminders or re-exposure is a major feature of PTSD (Yule & Gold 1993) (Kinchin 1992).

Physiological reactivity on exposure to cues of the event

Physiological reactivity might be described thus: a teenager is taking part in a lifesaving course at the local swimming pool. All is proceeding according to plan until the instructor suggests getting into the water wearing clothes to simulate real-life situations. For the teenager who survived the capsizing of the Herald of Free Enterprise this mirrors the trauma she experienced and she may start to react to this reminder. The trigger or cue for this teenager was not swimming, it was wearing wet clothing. The response is as if she were back on the capsizing ferry. She clambers as high as she can to get away from the water and studies the roof over the swimming pool as if seeking out a rescue helicopter.

Triggers for panic attacks can vary greatly. The stimuli may involve aspects such as smell, sound, texture, or a trick of the light. The list of potential triggers is as long as the list of potential traumas. For a person standing in a crowded lift this may be a reminder of a playground bullying incident. Smells in the school chemistry laboratory may remind a child of a motoring accident in which a car overturned and battery acid was spilled onto the hot engine. The stabbing of Caesar in a Shakespearean production might bring back memories of a mugging which was witnessed many years earlier. Some reactions to situations will take the victim by surprise, adding to the distress brought about by the reactivation of the traumatic memory.

Efforts to avoid thoughts, feelings, activities, places or people associated with the event

It is logical for people who have been traumatised to protect themselves from situations which may prolong the traumatic memory. To do this, they may intentionally avoid thoughts or feelings, and make concerted efforts to avoid activities or situations that might trigger any recollection of the event.

This avoidance might focus on everyday activities such as refusing to get into a car (but being quite happy to travel by bus). It could be a refusal to attend college, or to attend certain lessons whilst at college, or perhaps a refusal to stand in a queue or attend church because of the crowded atmosphere. A child who is being bullied may refuse to attend school or an employee who is being repeatedly harassed may refuse to go to work. These are sometimes misdiagnosed as 'school phobia' or 'work phobia'

On one level, the refusal to discuss an event can be seen as avoidance. This is not a stubborn refusal to talk (which might be the case in other circumstances) but an agitated, and distressed refusal. (A genuine inability to remember should not be considered a refusal to talk.) Avoidance strategies might be obvious such as the use of alcohol or drugs to 'cloud' the traumatic memory. Overwork is sometimes used as a strategy to avoid thoughts and feelings about the trauma and although this behaviour might more usually be attributed to adults, it is not uncommon in adolescents, and even occurs in some children.

Sometimes the survivor is aware of the strategy being employed, but at other times they are unaware of the reason behind particular actions other than the knowledge that to proceed would be distressing and frightening.

Inability to recall an important aspect of the event

It is common for people who suffer head injuries, or "blackouts" (which may or may not be the consequence of alcohol or drug abuse), to be unable to remember events or to have a memory failure. Lack of ability to recall the event is not part of the criterion for PTSD in this context.

The "psychogenic amnesia" which is reported by traumatised people is an inability to recall particular aspects of the trauma or its immediate aftermath. John LeCarré explains this wonderfully in his novel *Tinker, Tailor, Soldier, Spy.* He writes, "There are moments which are made up of too much stuff for them to be lived at the time they occur."

During a traumatic incident a person's senses are working overtime. Sight, sound, smell, taste and touch are all channelling information as fast as they can and the victim's brain is trying to cope with this. It is quite natural therefore, that some of the information is not assimilated and stored in the memory. A child who survives a road accident in which his mother is killed might not remember being told that 'mummy is dead'. A woman who is being assaulted at knife point might not hear the sirens of the police car coming to her assistance and she might not recognise police officers - despite their uniform.

There is so much going on during the trauma that it is impossible to memorise everything. There wasn't time for this to happen. Anecdotally, it is memories related to sounds which are most often missing.

Markedly diminished interest in significant activities

The essential feature of this symptom is a lowering of interest in previously enjoyed events. However, for the symptom to occur the activities which are no longer of interest must have been very significant to the survivor prior to the trauma. The diminishing interest must not be part of what would otherwise be considered a normal developmental change.

A boy who was keen on football and a regular player in the school team would not usually be expected to stop playing football immediately after a boating accident. A woman who could not keep her nose out of books, prior to a trauma, would not generally be expected to ignore the written word in favour of idly watching television following the death of her baby. In both of these stereotypical examples the victim has abandoned an activity which was a part of their previous life - not just a passing interest.

In some cases avoidance might almost be seen as the survivor punishing themselves, by abstaining from something they previously relished. It is a way of coming to terms with their trauma and survival.

Feelings of detachment

Once again, the essence of this symptom is that a person's character has changed after the trauma. If they were described as a 'bit of a loner' prior to the trauma then it might be difficult to apply this description following a traumatic incident. Some folk prefer their own company.

A child from a family with a strong religious background might find that going to church after the death of her brother ceased to have meaning. She might feel alone and alienated, receiving no comfort and perceiving that her faith has betrayed her. She now attends church out of habit alone. This behaviour would not have been normal for her prior to the trauma.

The same might also apply to a teenager who attended a youth club and felt the support and friendship of the club and its leaders. However, following the witnessing of a serious car accident, she no longer entered into the spirit of the club, but just sat in the corner drinking coffee and smoking cigarettes. She no longer sought out her friends or the youth leader with whom she previously had a very strong (but appropriate) friendship.

Graham:

I spend much of my day at home, alone. My wife is out at work during the week. At weekends I like to go swimming, or walking, or cycling. I like to do things that involve me being on my own. That way there are no awkward questions. I don't have to think about anything complicated - I just drift. I don't think I even enjoy the exercise.

If I were a car, I would be coasting down the road out of gear. I wouldn't turn left or right, I'd just travel on, and on, and on.

The result of this emotional 'switch-off' is that the victim will avoid crowds, avoid friends, avoid fun, and avoid all the things that make life enjoyable. It all becomes too much effort and too risky. It is much safer to curl up and watch the world go by, paint a watery smile on your face, and feel nothing inside. This is known as the numbing phase of PTSD. It is a period of detachment and isolation which has to be broken.

Sense of a foreshortened future

If a person has experienced a serious threat to their life, and they have almost been killed, they may suddenly become very aware that life is fragile and limited. Therefore, some trauma victims may not expect to have a career, or a marriage or children of their own. They are no longer surprised by the thought that they might not live to old age. They are not likely to engage in saving for future events, or pension plans.

This is not the same as a person who has no regard for their actions and becomes amoral as a consequence and says, "So what if I get arrested - who cares?" That is not a sense of foreshortened future. That is an irresponsible attitude.

Sleep difficulties

Sleep difficulties are divided into two groups: those people who have trouble falling asleep, and those who have difficulty staying asleep. If sleep is going to produce nightmares then many survivors will not want to fall asleep since that is a way of preventing the frightening dreams from happening.

Children often regress in sleep patterns, wanting to sleep with a light on, or in a room with someone else, or even in bed with their parents. Clock-watching, or appearing to be awake all night and watching the clock tick slowly round, but benefiting from a series of short naps is quite common. However, this is often reported as very poor quality sleep and people who clock-watch are often tired during the day.

Cindy:

I was getting very bad tempered. I was tired and suffered with frequent headaches. I thought the bump on the head had upset my ability to sleep. I was always wide awake by 4 am. In the end I became obsessed with not sleeping. It dominated my thoughts. I blamed everything on being tired and not sleeping very well. I even got a new bed!

Occasionally, this symptom is reversed and survivors have no difficulty sleeping - the problem becomes managing to stay awake. It is possible that constant sleeping could be a form of avoidance behaviour. Or, in the case of bullying and abuse, it may be exhaustion from the constant activation of the fight or flight response, the drain on emotional energy, and the effort involved in healing.

Irritability or outbursts of anger

It is not surprising that PTSD survivors experience periods of general irritability and are at risk of suddenly losing their tempers over trivial matters. There is an awareness of the loss of control during angry outbursts which may be similar to any loss of control during the original trauma. Following such an outburst there is often a period of embarrassment and apology.

Christine:

I just exploded. All that happened was that my eldest daughter smashed a plate while washing-up. It was the last straw. I went on and on at her for being so stupid. My husband intervened and tried to take hold of me by the shoulder. I swung around and hit him, hard, across the face.

We stood looking at each other for a few seconds, then I collapsed in floods of tears. Such a simple accident had become a major conflict. It was out of all proportion. I'd lost the plot.

Difficulty concentrating and remembering

Trauma survivors frequently report great difficulty concentrating when they attempt simple tasks. Students asked to concentrate on classroom teaching, or on computations or reading may find great difficulty in applying themselves to the task. This may partly be due to the intrusive images which occupy their thoughts.

Survivors may also experience difficulties remembering details such as their mobile phone number or email address.

They may forget the route home from work. Circumstances which can be explained as simple absent-mindedness in older people is extremely frustrating and vexing to all survivors.

Hypervigilance

A person who has been mugged will pay excessive attention to what is going on around him. This is not a general suspiciousness of situations. It is a detailed and persistent search for any clues which might alert the survivor to further trouble of any description.

Survivors will often study people if they are within close proximity. They are seeking out potential dangers. Survivors may well stand with their backs to walls to limit the number of directions from which potential dangers can arrive. The level of vigilance is 'hyper', that is, far beyond that required from a realistic appraisal of the situation.

Arlette:

I was so jumpy it wasn't true. I used to panic waiting for the morning post. I knew it was due to arrive, but would always jump out of my skin when the spring in the letter box snapped shut.

Exaggerated startle response

Survivors may be disturbed by any sudden noise or movement. In this case the individual may exhibit a startle response which is disproportionate to both the stimulus and behaviour which would normally be expected in such circumstances.

Developmental regression (in children)

Young children may regress developmentally following a trauma. Anecdotal evidence suggests that this regression might be by as much as two to three years and may be observed by the way a child plays, eats, sleeps or seeks attention. Thumb-sucking, baby talk, drinking from a bottle, returning to the support of a previously discarded 'cuddly' toy and bed-wetting are the most obvious signs that a young child's development is in temporary regression (Scott & Palmer 2000). Recently acquired skills may become lost and children may show clinging behaviour, not wanting to leave a parent in the mornings and not wanting to leave school at the end of the day.

N.B. All of these behaviours (clinging, thumb sucking etc.) are normal behaviours and should only be considered as symptoms of PTSD if the child regresses to this behaviour, having previously outgrown it.

Physical pains

Many survivors may appear to be suffering from physical injuries. Although not physically hurt they may experience back pains, muscle cramps or severe headaches. The causes of these pains will probably be psychosomatic, but the pain they feel is real and may require treatment in its own right.

Depression

Survivors commonly report significantly high rates of depression (Yule 1999). They may have strong suicidal thoughts and take overdoses in the year after the trauma. A significant number become very anxious after accidents.

In the light of the other symptoms, feelings of depression and anxiety should be expected and anticipated. Life has changed and the future no longer looks rosy.

Chapter four

Families, friends and faith

At the centre of any traumatic incident are the victims and the rescuers. These people are surrounded by a network of family and friends. It follows, therefore, that those people are also going to be affected by the traumatic incident. They become secondary victims of Post Traumatic Stress Disorder.

PARTNERS

Like bereavement, traumatic responses can have both positive and negative consequences. Some couples will be drawn closer together. They share the concerns and worries of their partners. Their need for each other will deepen. Other couples may find themselves drifting apart, maybe searching for a less demanding and more shallow relationship. Recovery from PTSD is a painful experience for all of them.

Whichever way you look at the situation, the partners of PTSD sufferers are in for a difficult time. There are few short cuts and plenty of rows, interspersed with occasional successes.

The relationship can feel uneasy because life has suddenly shown how unpredictable it can be. In the aftermath of the trauma this is quite understandable, and allowances can be made for the erratic mood of the victim. With time, however, the level of understanding can diminish, and what was originally considered to be erratic behaviour becomes misinterpreted as sheer bloody-mindedness.

A reluctance to discuss things can become a source of friction in a relationship. It is often the case that PTSD sufferers are unwilling to discuss the trauma with their partner, but are more inclined to impart the details to friends. Such behaviour might be mistaken for a lack of trust, but it is more to do with protecting those closest to them. Some victims have found that they can sit in the local bar and tell friends how close they came to death but would be unable to relate the same story at home, alone, with their partner. This 'protection' of the partner is very common and lasts only a short time in most cases. However, it does give rise to feelings of rejection. The partner feels excluded from some part of the loved-one's life. Do not put undue pressure on your partner to tell everything in one go. You will get the full story, but it might be delivered in small, more manageable chapters.

Money can be a source of constant anxiety and worry. Many PTSD victims are unable to work for a long period of time. This lack of employment will inevitably be reflected in financial straits within the family. In these cases, money is a frequent topic of conversation, and a constant reminder that all is not well. Financial problems bring pressure to return to work quickly. Often this can force a premature return to work with the inevitable consequence that more time off work will be required at a later date. State benefits, company welfare, and insurance policies can lessen the financial blow to many families, but the problem never really goes away.

Sex often becomes an issue between partners. Either one or both can discover an increased or decreased physical desire. On top of all the other changes going on at the time, this variation in sexual appetite will be an added strain. Partners may start to search for a reason for this change and there may be feelings of insecurity as the change is inflicted upon the relationship speedily. Worries about sexual faithfulness may grow if partners find themselves becoming sexually incompatible. This all adds up to increased strain at a time when the relationship needs some extra flexibility.

It is difficult to maintain a close personal relationship when your thoughts are constantly interrupted by images of a life-threatening, traumatic situation. Many veterans of war have found it impossible to remain in such a relationship while continuing to mourn the deaths of those colleagues who were close to them. It is important to take professional advice before the changes inflicted by the trauma impose an irreversible situation.

Jessica:

I knew the wives of several war veterans. They told me that their husbands occasionally just shut them out of their lives. They would drift off into their own thoughts and ignore the family around them. I realised I sometimes felt like that. I had never been anywhere near a war, but my feelings were similar to the veterans. I wanted to be alone. I didn't want to be touched or cuddled. I didn't want to talk. I just shut my husband out.

With so much changing, panic is a natural reaction. In the case of PTSD victims and their partners, this may show itself as bouts of excessive spending. When a life-plan has suddenly been turned upside-down it can lead to feelings of 'let's spend, and enjoy it while we can'. Although the occasional treat is fully justified, squandering life savings in a matter of weeks is invariably a great mistake. Such whims, which will only add further difficulties to the process of recovery from the trauma, must be guarded against.

Another issue which is likely to unsettle partners is a change in lifestyle. A partnership may develop a new approach, perhaps with the other partner taking the lead. This can be a simple matter of who drives the car, or it might be that the role of major breadwinner has passed from one partner to the other. This new way of life, or new image, will take time to adapt to. There may be conflicts within the partnership, particularly when the victim wishes to regain control over aspects of life which had temporarily become the responsibility of the other partner.

This situation may build up all sorts of anger and frustration which can be directed at anything or anyone when the explosion finally comes. Both partners must be made aware of what is taking place.

The inability to make even the simplest decisions can become infuriating. Constant preoccupation with the incident, the keeping of scrapbooks and diaries, can appear to be shutting the other partner out of this part of life.

Changes in mood can often catch partners out. Moods may suddenly swing from contentedness to disorientated confusion, then to total loss of interest in a short space of time. Nightmares and dreams can also be disturbing for partners.

Shame and fear about behaviour, plus avoidance of anything to do with the incident can drastically restrict family life. Activities which were once popular may suddenly become a thing of the past.

Graham:

Things that I used to think important have lost that importance in my life. My car needed new tyres. I knew that it was risky driving on the existing set, but I just didn't care. I drove around for about three months like that. Every time I saw a police car I felt guilty, but I still did not change them.

Eventually my wife noticed them. I got a real earful from her for not doing anything about it. I just threw her the keys and told her to do it herself. That sort of thing had always been one of my jobs around the house.

She just stared at me, walked out and slammed the door. I watched her drive down the road with tears running down her cheeks. I felt terrible about it.

When she returned we had a cuddle and I said how sorry I was. She explained that she had actually quite enjoyed her change in role. Going to the garage and pricing a set of tyres was a new experience for her.

Partners of PTSD victims should feel able to seek help in their own right. If they have problems coping, or sleeping, or even understanding the issues around PTSD then partners should make an appointment to see their GP, just like any other person with a medical anxiety.

CHILDREN AND PARENTS

It is sometimes impossible for children to express their feelings about a traumatic event. That does not mean they are unaffected. Adults frequently underestimate a child's level of understanding of complicated issues (Kinchin & Brown 2001). This underestimation is a positive hindrance when assessing how children have been affected by a family trauma (see Chapter 8).

Added to this complication is the child's natural inquisitiveness and ability to catch snatches of adult conversations. In consequence, the child may perceive the trauma to be even more dramatic than it already is. The truth may hurt initially, but in the long term a policy of honesty is more likely to ease the situation.

"Daddy's not very well" or "Mummy's had a bit of a shock" are not adequate explanations for adults. Why should they be adequate for children?

Matthew:

Working with children for most of the day, I have come to understand just how tough they are. Many of them wanted to talk about death. Most had experienced someone close to them dying.

Following John's death, I found that I had developed a greater understanding of what these children had been telling me. I realised that their perception of death, and its consequences, was often very mature.

I never actually told them about John's death. That would not have been right. But I think they sensed that I really did understand what they were telling me.

However, some issues are beyond the comprehension of very young children. The trauma of being raped means very little to a three-year-old. In such situations, a simplified version of the trauma must be prepared. Not a lie, but a simple version of the truth.

HOW DO CHILDREN COPE?

Children don't sit down and talk about their worries and troubles (Saylor 1993). They incorporate their fears into their play and their attitudes to others. They may become uncharacteristically aggressive towards their peers. Their games may develop themes which involve conflict and aggression: war games, criminal actions or violent accidents may all be acted out. The aggression may become explosive in nature, making the child unpopular at a time when friends are necessary.

Child primary victims of PTSD tend to show fear and are easily startled (Kinchin & Brown 2001). They have a disturbed sleep pattern and exhibit signs of guilt and depression. Occasionally these children will switch off, becoming disengaged from their surroundings, and their return to the present may precipitate an act of aggression.

Children who become secondary victims of PTSD, because of a traumatic event experienced by a close family member, may well experience the same symptoms. Because of the difficulty in establishing support groups for child PTSD sufferers, it is frequently hard to set up satisfactory counselling for these young victims of trauma.

The parents of PTSD victims also have a tough time. This includes both parents of young victims and parents of adult PTSD sufferers. In many families the parent-child bond remains close. In others, the trauma may drive a wedge through that close bond. An uneasiness develops in the relationship. Things become less easy to talk about. Silences become strained. In these instances, somebody must take the lead. The PTSD victim should be given every opportunity to talk, but should not be coerced into talking. It is natural for the victim to wish to protect parents from the awful reality of what has happened. Viewed from the parents' side, this may feel like being shut out, and it may hurt. Opportunities to discuss the trauma and the fears should be provided. Once the victim starts to talk, there will probably be no stopping him, but it may be some time before the moment feels right. Patience is required.

FRIENDS AND WORK MATES

PTSD can stretch friendship to the very limit. It is a difficult time for the friends and colleagues of a victim. They feel that they must do something, but find that when they cannot do anything there is an overwhelming sense of failure. Friends are not usually trained in counselling, but they already have the trust and friendship of the victim. In these circumstances, it is not surprising that many victims find it easier to talk to a friend in a way that they have been unable to talk to partners and close relatives.

The same is true for those colleagues who are in a position of leadership or authority (Raphael 1986). When faced with the task of consoling a PTSD victim, they may feel that they should have the solutions to particular problems. They are used to formulating plans of action and are confused when faced with such a complex emotional condition. Simply visiting the victim can eventually be thought to be a futile exercise because it isn't actually doing anything.

It is at times of crisis that you find out exactly what your friendship and comradeship is worth. Some friends will stick by you, others will fade away into the background. Stick with those who stand by you. They are real friends who clearly value your company and want to help. They may not know how to help you, but cannot be criticised for trying. It is a tough time in any friendship.

Friends and colleagues can help by:
- being there
- showing that they care
- developing the skills of a good listener
- trying to understand how trauma affects individuals
- offering help with practical problems

Of course, partners and family can also do all of the above, but because of their closeness to the victim they are involved in the care process more extensively and so will benefit from the 'break' that friends will be able to offer.

Arlette:

The doctor told me to talk it over with my partner or a friend. But I'd got to the stage where I didn't know who my friends were. I was so confused by the situation I found myself talking to the furniture!

There are occasions when either family or friends are actively involved in the trauma itself. This can be an advantage, or a major problem. It is common in instances of sexual abuse for the guilty party to be a family member, maybe even a parent. This may result in the victim shutting out the rest of the family until it is established who can be trusted. In cases of sexual abuse, this is a serious dilemma for the victim, and such a situation can cause the break-up of the entire family if outside help is not quickly sought.

Family, friends or colleagues may have shared the traumatic experience with the PTSD victim. This shared experience may make it easier for those involved to discuss the event and work through the stresses of the situation in a type of group therapy. It may also have the opposite effect. 'We went through this together, why has it not affected him the same way it affected me?' In this situation, feelings of guilt, failure, embarrassment and detachment may make discussion of the event virtually impossible.

Families can suffer if they are unable to approach the issues correctly. Families with trauma victims may be more inclined to outbursts of anger and violence. Their care skills and ability to be intimate may dwindle as poor communication leads to lack of trust and feelings of insecurity. A general dissatisfaction with life may become the predominant family mood. Victims are hard to cheer up, and can be prone to repeated recurrences of crisis and panic. Substance abuse and sexual dissatisfaction are problems which may occur.

There are some instances where the whole family has been traumatised by the event and so cannot help each other. Natural and man-made disasters have a habit of affecting entire families. The Aberfan and Buffalo Creek disasters, mentioned in the opening chapter, are prime examples.

Even the families with the very best coping strategies will need outside help at times like this.

FAITH

Many PTSD victims turn to their faith as a comfort at a time of need. For some who previously had little religious faith, it can be a great time of discovery as they explore something new.

Many churches contain members who can be good "listeners" at a time of crisis. They are not necessarily trained counsellors, but they have compassion and understanding and will sit and listen without passing judgement. For many, such listeners can be a middle-ground between telling members of the family, and talking to a professional counsellor. In this way, many people have found comfort and an inner peace. Talking about your problems to a sincere and sympathetic listener can be a great help.

As an aid to those who wish to turn to religion for comfort, I have included the text of a well-known prayer. The prayer of St. Francis has comforted many people for almost eight hundred years, and the words are particularly poignant for those who have experienced trauma in their lives.

PRAYER OF ST. FRANCIS

Lord, make me an instrument of your peace:
    where there is hatred let me sow love,
    where there is injury let me sow pardon,
    where there is doubt let me sow faith,
    where there is despair let me give hope,
    where there is darkness let me give light,
    where there is sadness let me give joy.
O Divine Master, grant that I may
    not try to be comforted but to comfort,
    not try to be understood but to understand,
    not try to be loved but to love.
Because it is in giving that we receive,
it is in forgiving that we are forgiven,
and, it is in dying that we are born to eternal life.

ST. FRANCIS 1209 AD

Arlette:

As one door closes, another slams right in your face. That is how it felt to me. I just went from bad to worse. Everything went wrong for me. I trusted nobody. Then, I just happened to say something to someone at church. Doors started to open again.

Finally, the prayer 'To Healing' was sent to me by a person recovering from PTSD. Following her attendance at PTSD workshops I facilitated, we grew to understand each others needs. She confessed to not liking the prayer from St Francis but used that prayer as an inspiration to write her own, which is reproduced here with her blessing and full permission.

To Healing

God of all potential goodness,
Revive my sickened heart to pulsate with gently flowing
   peace.
Where there is hatred, let me somehow find caring;
Where there is injury, healing;
Where there is doubt, validation of the truth;
Where there is despair, hope;
Where there is darkness, light;
Where there is sadness, joy.
Grant that I may find
strength and support in mutual comfort;
warmth in human commonality;
understanding of my deepest, unique, unknown self, and
love that I can feel, nurture and invest in giving.

Help me to discover a safe path
Where upon I may freely progress
With energy and empowerment
To transcend the overwhelming pain and awareness of our
innate weakness,
vulnerability and inhumanity.
Lead me to a new life that will be mine to claim
As an acceptance and acceptable entitlement -
A life where I may feel
Welcome
To joyfully choose to share ...

G.V.M. 2000 AD

Chapter five

Complications

Those who suffer from Post Traumatic Stress Disorder have to negotiate an obstacle course in order to recover. It is necessary to examine in detail some of the hurdles that must be faced.

Complicating factors in PTSD are:
- panic
- depression
- alcoholism
- drug abuse
- adverse publicity
- ignorance of PTSD
- relapses in recovery
- physical and sexual abuse

PANIC

Attacks of panic can be extremely frightening, and exhausting. Recovery from a severe panic attack can take a considerable time - days rather than hours. So what happens when people say they are suffering from a panic attack?

Following the traumatic event, certain sights, smells or sounds may spark off an instant warning that the event is about to be repeated. These 'triggers' are misinterpreted by the brain, and chemical messages within the body prepare you for a 'fight or flight' situation. If these triggers present themselves frequently, the brain repeats the messages and the body lunges from one panic to another.

The features of a panic attack vary from person to person, but some of the effects are common to most sufferers. The heart rate increases and breathing becomes more laboured. Some people start to pant, taking their breath in short, frequent gasps. Muscles, particularly in arms and legs, tighten and this causes considerable pain. In some instances people complain that their vision becomes clouded or blurred. Other people are convinced that they are going to faint. Occasionally, chest tightness and arm pains can become so intense that sufferers think they are having a heart attack. Such thoughts just add further fuel to the panic attack.

People in a state of panic are continually scanning their surroundings in a search for possible threats to their well-being. This is hypervigilance in the extreme.

In fact, collapsing or fainting is most unlikely. Panic alters the blood pressure in the opposite direction to that needed for fainting. The feelings of light-headedness (which might also affect vision) arise simply because more oxygen is being pumped to the muscles (ready for fight or flight) and less is going to the brain.

Panic attacks can also cause worry and anxiety for those around you. They might think you are having some kind of fit, or a heart attack, and consequently, they might unintentionally make matters worse.

If you find yourself in a panic situation the easiest remedy is to remove yourself from the source of panic. Easy to say, but not always easy to achieve. Some people find themselves panicking whilst on public transport. However, if you are on your way home from work, are you going to get out and walk, or try to sit out the attack?

Paul:

Sitting in a coach, immediately behind the driver, I should have felt safe. I could see what was going on ahead. I knew every single person on the coach. We had all been on the same outing.

I felt the panic start. My fists clenched and my arms went as rigid as steel. I started to breathe more rapidly and I could feel my heart pounding inside my chest. I closed my eyes and tried to concentrate on my breathing. I had to fight off this panic.

It just got worse and worse. In the end they stopped the coach and I got out to walk around. I don't know what everyone thought about me. I looked like a drug addict suffering from withdrawal symptoms. I was shaking and sweating, and very unsteady on my feet.

The real problem was that I knew I had to get back on the coach to travel home. I felt so trapped and frightened. As I climbed back onto the coach I knew I was in for two hours of hell - but there was nothing I could do about it.

If you concentrate on your breathing and slow your breathing down, then the panic will start to lessen. A panic attack is a vicious cycle of stimuli and responses. What you have to try to do is break that circle of events by removing one or the other. By concentrating on your breathing pattern (response) and slowing your breathing down, it is possible to break the circle.

Breathe in slowly . . . counting as you do so . . . one, two, three, four, five. Then breathe out in much the same way . . . one, two, three, four, five, six. This technique makes you concentrate on the mechanics of breathing and distracts from the panic. It is helpful if someone with you can enforce the counting. If you are on your own you must try to do this yourself.

The other way of dealing with a panic attack is to remove the stimulus that caused the initial panic. This is sometimes easier and is a short-term solution, but it does mean that sooner or later you will have to face up to that stimulus once again.

David:

What happens when the phone rings? First, I panic. I get hot and start to sweat. My breathing quickens and becomes less effective. My muscles tense up. If it is a particularly bad panic attack, my vision blurs, I become dizzy and I can hear my own pulse. It becomes impossible to pick up the telephone receiver. Rarely do I wonder who is calling (Kinchin 1992).

Panic attacks should not be taken lightly. Learn from your experiences and do not set tasks which are doomed to fail and distress you. Some people will advise that you can 'flood' yourself with the situation or object that causes panic. In that way, you will eventually overcome the fear and end the panic. This 'flooding' is an antiquated idea which was clearly devised by someone who had never suffered a panic attack. It could possibly be dangerous. It will certainly be exhausting and, if it fails, you might find yourself with an even greater fear of that stimulus. The flooding technique should be avoided by all PTSD sufferers.

Panic attacks are at their worst when they are triggered unexpectedly. As part of their treatment, many PTSD sufferers will be exposed to situations which cause panic attacks, but in a controlled way. Unfortunately, life is unpredictable and occasionally the circumstances which cause the panic will present themselves unexpectedly. The suddenness of this will intensify the panic attack, and it is this unplanned exposure to stimuli which often causes the most acute panic response. Because of this risk, PTSD victims tend to become very wary of new or untried situations.

Matthew:

I was a little on edge, but the train was almost empty. In my carriage there was just one other passenger. It was my first trip to London - my first trip to Europe since John's death.

Then, at Shepherd's Bush, a drunk got on and sat opposite me. He looked me up and down (posh suit and airline bag) and came out with the classic opener, 'What U ... staring at?'

I looked away.

'You, c..., I asked you a question.'

I found a fascinating advert on the wall to examine in detail.

'Too posh to talk to me are you? Say something, even if it is .... off.'

Tempting!

I looked at him.

'I don't really have anything to say.' I was amazed how calm my voice was. Inside I was panicking and just wanted to get out. Silly idea to use the tube anyway. The carriage suddenly felt full and very small.

Ladbroke Grove.

'You're ... frightened of me, are you?'

'No.' I realised I was not at all frightened of him, but was terrified of my surroundings.

'You make me ... sick, you Yanks,' he stated bluntly. He stood up and staggered towards me.

I stood up quickly.

I stepped to one side; his fist missed me. I then punched him really hard on the side of his mouth.

Paddington.

The doors opened and I charged out.

There are no short solutions to the treatment of panic attacks. Those sufferers who want to conquer their feelings of panic must have a finely-scheduled timetable of actions and tasks to grade their exposure to the situation that causes panic.

DEPRESSION

Only a person who has been so down that he has contemplated ending his own life can truly understand such deep feelings of despair and depression. You are likely to feel frightened, have difficulty sleeping and remembering simple things; because your poor concentration limits the number of things you can do, it is only to be expected that gloomy feelings and despair will emerge. Many PTSD sufferers will experience periods of depression.

Jessica:

You feel isolated and very much alone - even in a crowded room. Life is no longer worth anything. There is no God, nobody cares and nothing has any purpose any more. It's frightening.

Depression, as a feature of PTSD, is a constellation of different symptoms - a syndrome - so that not every depressed PTSD sufferer will have the same symptoms. Some of the most common symptoms of depression that are linked to PTSD are:

- depressed mood most of the day, and nearly every day
- little interest or pleasure in any activity
- insomnia
- loss of energy nearly every day
- diminished ability to think clearly
- bouts of sadness, tearfulness or anger
- loss of interest in sex/food
- preoccupation with guilty feelings
- reduced concentration
- feelings of worthlessness/hopelessness
- recurrent thoughts of death/suicide.

If at least half of these symptoms can be applied to your present state of mind, then you are probably suffering from depression.

Overcoming these depressive feelings requires considerable effort and help. Do not be afraid to seek help. Trying to cope with depression on your own can be dangerous. Help does not need to come from official medical sources such as family doctors or counsellors. Help can be gleaned from family and close friends. Firstly, YOU must acknowledge that you are feeling gloomy and that you want to do something to overcome those feelings. Admit the problem, there is no disgrace attached to it - you are not on trial. Then, you can start to seek out the solution.

If you feel that life has lost its flavour, then you must slowly start to re-establish things. Try to relax a little. Stop worrying about things over which you have no control. Concentrate on the things which you can change.

Question your reasons for feeling depressed:

- You might be feeling guilty. Are you being over-critical of yourself?
- You may consider that you are worthless. You are not.
- You may have a very low self-esteem. List your achievements.
- You may feel unloved. Look around at the people who care for you.

The list could go on. You must start to look at things in a positive way. When you look at a bottle of wine and notice that some of the contents have been drunk - say to yourself, 'This bottle is still half full.' Resist the thought that it is half empty. Think positively.

For those who are extremely depressed there is no substitute for professional advice and care. This might mean a course of therapy, or medication to see you through the crisis, because crisis is what it is. Resorting to medication is not a sign of failure. Refusing to acknowledge that you require outside help is the failing.

In some instances, depression is the first symptom of Post Traumatic Stress Disorder to present itself. In these cases it is important to acknowledge that the trauma you have suffered previously may be linked to the negative feelings you are experiencing now. Before the depression can be effectively treated, the trauma will have to be explored through counselling. Dealing with the trauma in this way will often significantly ease the depression.

ALCOHOLISM

People with problems often resort to drinking. It happens in the movies all the time. 'What you need is a stiff drink!' There is nothing wrong with the occasional stiff drink. Alcohol does relax people, and being able to relax is necessary. However, if the drinks are regular it will not be long before the only way you can relax is with a drink. Such a situation is the first step towards alcoholism.

Cindy:

I started drinking when I was about fifteen. After the accident I got fed up with everyone and started drinking even more. I would take bottles up to my room and drink the lot. It was costing me too much. That is when I realised exactly how much I was drinking.

Alcohol is handy for those people who cannot spontaneously disassociate themselves from events. It helps you to forget. It is no coincidence that the doctors portrayed in M.A.S.H., the US TV series about the Korean War, built their own drinks still inside their tent. They drank in order to forget the war, to forget their loved ones back home (who they were missing) and to forget their misbehaving whilst they were away from their loved ones.

Using alcohol as a prop in this way can have only one outcome. You will become dependent upon it, just like any other drug addict. For a PTSD sufferer to have to break an addiction too, is asking a great deal. The addiction will have to be successfully treated before the PTSD can be tackled, even though the PTSD may initially have been responsible for the alcoholism.

DRUG ABUSE

Much of what has been said about alcoholism is equally true of drug abuse. The main difference is that excessive drinking is (within reason) legal and more socially acceptable in some circles. But both addictions can be fatal.

Perhaps there is a difference here, according to age. Older PTSD sufferers may turn to drink, while younger sufferers may seek solace in drugs. Both groups are searching for a prop, something to help them through a difficult period in their lives. When people are desperate for help they will turn to anything or anyone who they think might be a source of comfort. Consequently, people who would never usually dream of using hard drugs find themselves purchasing illegal substances.

ADVERSE PUBLICITY
We live in an age dominated by the mass media. Newspapers, television and radio companies make considerable sums of money by selling news. Any incident which involves personal grief or tragedy is actively followed by the public, via the media.

Clearly, anyone involved in a large-scale, traumatic, potentially life-threatening situation is going to become a focus for media attention. Even if the people involved manage to escape direct attention, the event itself is likely to attract news-hunters and they will suffer indirectly.

Graham:
The press got hold of the story, and turned it all around. They said I crashed the car, and then some youths threw stones at it. They tried to make out it was all my fault. I suppose it made a better story.

Even those of us who have never suffered a traumatic incident will have witnessed such events in our homes, thanks to television.

What were you doing on 22 November last year? What were you doing on the day President John F. Kennedy was assassinated (22 November 1963)? Forty years later, many people can recall incidents from that day because they were so emotionally struck by the murder that was screened around the world.

Younger generations might well express the same sentiment about a much more recent incident which occurred on 31 August 1997. Princess Diana died in a high-speed car crash in Paris.

Because of their extensive, and almost instant, media coverage, people are brought to the scenes of major disasters whilst they are sitting in the security of their homes. This security is invaded so suddenly that we can often find our living rooms transformed into a disaster scene without any opportunity to prepare ourselves (Cohen 1991).

The pathetic sight of refugees and survivors; the devastation and destruction; the carnage. Film crews almost deliberately dwell on scenes that are going to tug on the emotions: a child's shoe; a toy; articles of clothing; a body. Such scenes can affect people who have no direct involvement other than watching a television screen.

Felicity:

It was November 1990, and I was watching some TV news film of Romanian orphans. The dark, wet, cold and smelly building they lived in was awful. I found tears running down my face. In a way, I felt as trapped as they were. They were victims, and I was a victim too. Seeing that piece of film made me realise I was trapped too. I cried a lot more than usual that night.

Sensationalising the news can do much damage to some survivors. It causes a deepening of the trauma, and often intrudes into private lives beyond the boundaries of acceptable behaviour.

The media have been instrumental in increasing public awareness of trauma. In consequence they have a great responsibility to bring news to the homes of millions, and to do this with a sympathetic and sensitive touch. What the media transmit influences the perceptions, attitudes and opinions of the world.

Publicity of any traumatic event usually has three stages. First, the event itself is covered in detail. The scale of the disaster will dictate how long this coverage might last. An air crash might be mentioned for just two or three news bulletins, and may appear in the newspapers in a couple of editions. A war, however, may dominate all media elements for months or years. This was the case during the Vietnam War and, more recently, the Falklands War, the Persian Gulf War and the conflict in Bosnia.

Other occasions when the media choose to highlight a traumatic incident are usually confined to any legal cases which are brought as a result of the event.

Paul:

I was sitting at home watching the news. Suddenly I saw a picture of the boat on its side. Floodlights showed people waving their arms to the rescuers. I thought I was going to see myself at any moment. I couldn't look - but I couldn't look away either. I was sweating and shaking. My girlfriend thought I was going to have a fit or something, but I couldn't talk to her.

Four years after the incident, seeing those pictures made the whole thing real once again.

Paul had seen this piece of film before, several times. It was the standard archive clip that the BBC screened every time the incident was mentioned. What made it so difficult was the unexpectedness of the film. A small, and rather technical, legal issue was being debated and the film was intended to provide visual impact to the argument. The impression such a sudden screening made on Paul was considerable. One moment he was sitting with his girlfriend in the safety of his own home. Then suddenly he was thrown emotionally backwards in time to the heart of the incident he was so busy trying to come to terms with. The sudden move from safety to danger resulted in the panic Paul felt.

This situation is common for any victim of a particularly newsworthy event. Time and time again, the same dramatic film clip will be produced to remind the rest of the audience what the traumatic event was like. Those who experienced the event first hand need no such reminders.

Anniversaries of events are often an excuse to show the same traumatic pictures again. Perhaps they are linked to the blessing of a memorial, or simply acting as a reminder to those unaffected by such tragedy. For the victims and the relatives of those who died, such anniversaries are painful occasions anyway. Even without visual reminders, those who are close to the event will be thinking about it on anniversaries. They may even seek out old press cuttings so as to check the accuracy of their own recollection of the event.

Marlene:

I opened up the scrap book and found the article from the local paper. They had an aerial photograph of the road junction, and a horrible picture of me wearing my nursing uniform. I read through the article, folded it back into the book and put it away again. The reporter wrote that the accident was my friend's fault. I have never believed that.

IGNORANCE OF PTSD / REFUSAL TO ACKNOWLEDGE THE DISORDER

The whole world was ignorant of Post Traumatic Stress Disorder prior to 1980. In one or two instances, however, communities were discovering that psychological trauma was equally as debilitating as any physical injury. These 'invisible injuries' were slowly starting to attract interest in the courts.

On both sides of the Atlantic, there were disasters which led to communities suffering greatly. In Aberfan the community was suffering grief brought about by the loss of so many young lives. In Buffalo Creek the residents were suffering similarly.

What helped increase the understanding of invisible injuries was the decision by over 600 survivors of the Buffalo Creek disaster to sue the Buffalo Mining Company (Stern 1976). To do this they had to obtain evidence to show that survivors of the incident suffered from psychological injuries. Lawyers started to seek ways of proving the existence of Post Traumatic Stress Disorder.

During World War I there were army officers who refused to believe there was such an illness as 'shell shock'. In their view, those soldiers claiming to be suffering from it were malingerers trying to find an excuse to be sent back home. Following the war Europe suddenly contained thousands of shell shocked victims, and even the great psychologist, Freud, acknowledged that these men were suffering from a 'profound reaction to the conflict'.

By the Second World War, 'war-neurosis' was a well-established condition, and in 1939 it was agreed that this condition could prove debilitating to soldiers. It was not considered to affect civilians, however.

Following the war in Vietnam the medical profession took the condition far more seriously, and by 1980 PTSD was well documented as an emotional condition. Unfortunately, after the war in the Persian Gulf there was a general reluctance by the governments of the European powers involved to admit that many, if any, combat veterans were suffering from PTSD. Some governments even refused to acknowledge that such a disorder even existed. Statistics were available on most other aspects of the conflict, but not on the incidence of Post Traumatic Stress.

Marlene:

In the army I met people who had served in Vietnam. You could be sitting and talking to them and suddenly you knew they were no longer listening. I used to think they were just bored. Now, I realise they were struggling to pay attention. Their mind was somewhere else. Their eyes were filled by images which were thousands of miles away.

Since my accidents I have thought about these veterans quite a bit. You see, I now have problems with attentiveness. I just switch off and my mind drifts on to other things. People must think I am so rude.

People who have been diagnosed as suffering from PTSD can often see symptoms of the disorder in others. However, most people think that being attentive is simply a matter of good manners. They cannot readily appreciate that there may be some medical reason why people appear to daydream. The ignorance about the problems faced by PTSD sufferers is overwhelming, and even extends to some doctors and health care workers.

David:

Before the police would let me retire I had to be examined by their medical officer. We sat and chatted for about thirty minutes and he concluded the medical by saying, 'I'm not sure about PTSD. You appear to have a sort of police phobia though.' Until that point, I thought he had understood me.

One of the most painful aspects of PTSD is the way that close family and friends react to the victim. Initially, there is plenty of support and understanding, but this becomes diluted by time. If, after several months, you are still showing signs of being unwell, you may find people becoming less sympathetic.

Richard:

During a police training exercise in which live petrol bombs were thrown, an instructor thought it would be a good idea to set himself alight, then act as though he was being badly burned. I was not expecting this, and had only just returned to work after the fire. I ended up by knocking him to the ground and smothering the flames with an emergency fire extinguisher which was nearby.

I was reprimanded for using the extinguisher. I should first have tried to use other means to halt the blaze. Despite my protests nobody understood that I just couldn't bear to see someone on fire for a second longer that I had to. They told me to pull myself together!

Sometimes sufferers feel that nobody really understands what they are experiencing. This can be an extremely lonely sensation which can lead back to feelings of depression and anxiety.

If the original trauma is of a private nature, these feelings of loneliness can become overwhelming. Victims of rape and sexual assaults don't usually tell many people about their trauma. In consequence, when they are seen to be behaving 'oddly' there are few people who can understand why, and make allowances for this behaviour.

All of a sudden, a friendly pat on the shoulder, or a hug, can take on a different meaning to those who have become very wary of any physical contact or closeness. Within marriages and partnerships these victims may experience problems in coping with, and enjoying, intimacy. Great understanding of their plight is required. They have to learn to trust again.

To try and rush these relationships will do great harm. To suggest that your partner is cold, or malingering, or manipulating the relationship will inevitably lead to furious and vicious rows. It may even lead to hatred. Remember that most women who experience rape see it as a life-threatening event, having feared mutilation or death during the assault (Herman 1992). Reintroducing any sexual experience is necessarily a task requiring patience, gentleness, love and understanding.

Christine:

It was three days before I could tell my husband anything. During that time I managed to avoid sex altogether. Once I told him, he was angry with everyone and we still avoided each other. It was nearly two weeks before I could even cuddle him in bed. He said he understood. But in his eyes I could see that he was not always sure of things.

RELAPSES IN RECOVERY

With many types of illness there is a standard rate of recovery. A common cold lasts a week. Broken ribs require six weeks before they stop aching. Other, more serious ailments may take several months. With PTSD, however, there is no precise timescale and this can often cause concern to those who are suffering. 'When will I be better?' turns into 'Will I ever recover?'

PTSD is diagnosed when the victim of trauma has been suffering for more than one month. If the symptoms last for longer than six months then the condition has become chronic. Beyond that, there is no real yardstick. Every case is different.

PTSD sufferers find themselves playing a game of emotional snakes and ladders. The game board is the road to recovery, divided into one hundred squares, and is covered by a series of ladders which help you on the way up. Between the ladders are the snakes which may take you backwards toward the start of the game. However, on a true snakes and ladders board no snake can take you all the way back to square one. This analogy is probably more realistic than the simple idea that recovery is a case of two steps forward and then one step back. Recovery is not that smooth, neither is it that predictable.

Many PTSD sufferers and their carers tend to set themselves goals or targets. Often these targets will be linked to the calendar:

- 'I will return to work by 1st June'
- 'I want to have stopped taking sleeping tablets by Christmas'
- 'I intend to go out shopping on my own during my holiday'

Formulating goals and targets is a good strategy provided the targets are within reach. If the target is too difficult, then you are setting yourself up to fail. That serves no useful purpose.

Set sensible, attainable, targets. Fix dates for accomplishing tasks which are a reasonable time away. If you reach the target before the date, then treat yourself - you have done well. Far better to do this than to set an almost impossible task and fail miserably. Inevitably, some targets are not going to be achieved. Life is full of unpredictable events and something will always happen that is likely to knock you off course. That's life! Allow for the unexpected in your preparation of targets. Give yourself a breathing space in your planning. Do not try to rush your recovery by setting target dates which you cannot reasonably be expected to reach.

Chapter six

PTSD and abuse

Child abuse is typically described as physical (including neglect), emotional or sexual. The wording 'significant harm' in The Children Act 1989 has resulted in a shift away from determining the circumstances of abuse to ascertaining the effect of maltreatment or neglect on the child. Abuse transcends all cultural, religious or social settings and although a child may experience all manner of abuse, one type is usually dominant within the child's life. Surveys conducted in Great Britain and The United States suggest approximately one in every ten children has suffered abuse (Mallon, 1997) and that 13% of women and 8% of men have experienced some form of abuse by the time they are eighteen years of age.

The trauma of abuse has long-lasting effects on children with some researchers concluding sexual abuse causes the greatest damage (Draijer, 1994). If sexual abuse is combined with other abuse the effects are potentially extremely damaging. The severity of the abuse is a significant factor in determining the harm done to individual children. However many children suffer more than one form of maltreatment or neglect and it is often the accumulation of this that causes long-term harm.

Abused children frequently demonstrate behaviour associated with Complex PTSD which can overwhelm their coping responses. Schofield (1997) describes two levels of trauma response with different characteristics. The first type involves a single event and the child recalling in detail what happened. The second type concerns long-standing situations of maltreatment or abuse where the child may develop coping strategies. In these circumstances the child attempts to deny the event and they may create 'a daytime self' and 'a night-time self'.

The abuse category under which a child is registered as abused is a matter for professional judgement. However the definitions of abuse are those set out in The Children Act 1989 (Paragraph 6:40). An abuser is someone who aims at using the child as a means of his or her own satisfaction without regard for the child's wishes. Often the abuser will be in a care-taking position; be aware that what is happening is taboo; exert power over the child; deceive the child into believing what is happening is a result of the child's encouragement or behaviour; be aware of the child's fear.

The link between PTSD and both physical and sexual abuse is the subject of other texts (Smith 1989). However, the subjects are often so closely linked that it is unwise to discuss PTSD without at least mentioning abuse. In fact, of all the letters I received following the publication of the first edition of this book, over one third were from victims of physical and sexual abuse. Consequently, I decided to make this problem the subject of a chapter in its own right.

Some sufferers are PTSD victims as a direct result of abuse. This may be physical abuse or domestic battering. It may be sexual abuse such as rape or incest. There are also a number of people who have suffered traumatic, potentially life-threatening events, and who have a previous history of either physical or sexual abuse. There are studies which suggest that people who have previously been abused in some way are more likely to suffer from PTSD following a traumatic event. That does not mean that every PTSD victim has been the subject of such abuse, but some have.

Sexual abuse has no discrimination; it can occur to anyone. People of all ages, all social classes, all ethnic groups and both sexes have suffered from this kind of abuse. However, rape and sexual abuse are the only violent crimes in which women are more likely to become victims than men.

Examples of sexual abuse leading to PTSD

Wife battering	Husband battering	Child battering
Date rape	Gang rape	Rape in marriage
Incest	Prostitution	Child rape

Abuse of any kind may affect victims in a variety of ways. Clearly, their health will suffer. There may be physical injuries inflicted; there are almost certainly psychological (invisible) injuries sustained. For females, there is also the possibility of pregnancy; for both sexes there is the risk of having contracted sexually transmitted diseases, including the AIDS virus. Many abuse victims will experience the intrusive and physical symptoms of PTSD and will seek to become avoidant in their actions.

The victims will experience a whole range of feelings and emotions and may be unable to control their emotional swings. They may alternate between anger and fear, helplessness and vulnerability, sadness and depression, guilt and shame. They will experience feelings of being responsible for what has happened to them. Such an emotional turmoil is extremely confusing and difficult to control.

Some victims may experience a phenomenon known as the "Stockholm Syndrome" (Parkinson 1993). During a bank robbery in Stockholm in 1973 some people were held hostage by the robbers. During the traumatic incident the hostages developed feelings of admiration, sympathy and empathy with their captors. In turn, the captors developed a degree of sympathy and admiration for their hostages. This has since been repeated in other hostage situations and also has similarities with the relationship between the 'abused' and their 'abuser'.

The Stockholm Syndrome should not be confused with "trauma bonding" which exists only between fellow victims of traumatic situations.

It is possible that these feelings of sympathy are responsible for the ties of loyalty in cases of abuse and battering. It may be the main reason for some abuse situations becoming so prolonged. There is often a reluctance by the victim to expose the culprit for exactly what he or she is: a person who enjoys malicious acts which cause hurt and pain to others.

Prolonged abuse can have a devastating effect upon the lives of the victims. Basic daily activities and relationships can suffer. Formal education will be adversely affected in younger abuse victims. Adult abuse victims may struggle to maintain a satisfactory partnership, be poor parents, wrestle with their career and play a lesser part in community life than they would originally have wished. They may achieve less, earn less, contribute less in taxes, be in receipt of more benefits, and consume more medical and mental health resources than they would otherwise have done. Many victims allow the feelings of guilt and shame to dominate their lives.

PROLONGED TRAUMATIC STRESS
The betrayal of trust is a particular concern of the victims of prolonged abuse and bullying. Some psychologists have labelled these victims as suffering from PDSD (Prolonged Duress Stress Disorder) which is now more commonly referred to as Complex PTSD, as opposed to PTSD. The symptoms and treatment of the two disorders are almost identical, but the reason for the suffering is a series of distressing events rather than just one traumatic event. In the case of emergency service personnel it is sometimes difficult to ascertain whether they are suffering from PTSD following one traumatic event, or C-PTSD as a result of dealing with a whole series of distressing incidents.

TRUST
People who have been abused at the hands of others have difficulty in trusting again. Trust is especially important if you intend to discuss a traumatic event. When victims decide to disclose what has happened to them they have selected that person because they truly trust them. If that trust is betrayed, they will not be so ready to trust another person.

When looking for a person to trust, look for two attributes. Look for someone whose behaviour is predictable, and who has broadly similar values to your own.

Bully OnLine

validation • enlightenment • re-empowerment

www.bullyonline.org

Workplace bullying • School bullying
Family bullying • Related issues
Media contact and referral for targets of bullying
News • Case histories • Support groups
An answer to the question *Why me?*
How to recognise a serial bully
Stress • Injury to health • PTSD
Action to tackle bullying • Legal information
Books • Resources • Web links • Contacts

IS THIS HAPPENING TO YOU OR SOMEONE YOU KNOW?

Bullying is: constant criticism, nit-picking, fault-finding, undermining, isolation, exclusion, being singled out, marginalised, belittled, humiliated, shouted at, threatened, overloaded, your work and credit for it stolen, responsibility increased but authority taken away, leave refused, training denied, unrealistic goals and deadlines, worst jobs/shifts etc, hypocrisy, duplicity, fabrication, distortion, twisting everything you say and do, abuse of disciplinary procedures, imposition of verbal/written warnings for trivial reasons, unfair dismissal.

Bullying causes: stress, anxiety, sleeplessness, waking early, fatigue, trauma, tearfulness, irritability, anger, headaches, frequent illness, IBS, aches and pains, skin problems, poor concentration & memory, sweating, palpitations, panic attacks, obsessiveness, fear, embarrassment, shame, guilt, hypervigilance (feels like but is *not* paranoia), hypersensitivity, fragility, isolation, reactive depression, stress breakdown, shattered self-confidence, low self-esteem, family breakdown, etc.

The serial bully: Jekyll & Hyde nature, control freak, compulsive liar, charming, verbally facile, selective memory, devious, manipulative, evasive, spiteful, vengeful, arrogant, fraudulent, doesn't listen, can't sustain adult conversation, denies everything, lacks conscience, shows no remorse, is drawn to power, also cold, humourless, aggressive, disruptive, divisive, selfish, glib, insensitive, insincere, immature - *but always plausible.*

The predictable behaviour is necessary because when a trusted confidant says he will do something, or be somewhere at a specific time, you expect him to do that. If you are let down repeatedly by the person's unpredictable behaviour, then you are unlikely to be able to trust that person fully.

The second element of trust is having similar values. Are you in general agreement on the basic values of life? Do you both have the same degree of respect for other people? Do you both treat confidential information in the same way? Can you trust this person and tell them everything?

These are the questions in the mind of every person seeking counsel, but are even more dominant in the mind of an abused or battered person who may have been exploited as a result of trusting someone close to them on previous occasions: their abuser.

Victims of physical and sexual abuse are probably no more common today than they were thirty years ago. However, today victims are more likely to "whistle-blow" on their abuser because they know they will be treated with sympathy by the authorities. That was not always the case. A group of people who suffered sexual abuse have produced a collected work of their thoughts, words and pictures under the title of "The Memory Bird" (Malone 1996). One victim, Mary, has kindly allowed me to reproduce one of her poems on these pages.

The fact that a book like "The Memory Bird" can be printed today is a testament to the courage and the strength of those who have been so badly abused. Many of these people have been diagnosed as suffering from Post Traumatic Stress Disorder. I think that in most cases that diagnosis should be changed to Complex Post Traumatic Stress Disorder. I personally know of people who have been consistently sexually abused for well over twenty years. These survivors are truly courageous people.

Christine:

It was years before I trusted anyone, especially any men. Even now, I think twice before placing myself in any position where I am not in complete control of what is happening to me. It is terrible not to trust people, but I just can't help it. I've given up worrying about it now. I am sure that trust will return in time.

Oh me

Little me and big me
Old me and new me
First me and every me
Changing me
Rearranging me.

~

Real me and false me
Accepting me
The whole of me
Truly me
Wonderful me.

© 1996 Mary J McMahon

Christine is not alone in being reluctant to trust people. It is a common symptom of those who have been abused and of those who have been bullied. This is particularly troublesome when it comes to forging new relationships. There is no easy solution to overcoming the problem of trust, but I think that those who contributed to the writings of "The Memory Bird" have taken a positive step towards trusting others once again.

The biennial Comic Relief awareness days, known more affectionately as Red Nose Days, are another attempt to raise awareness of the abuse children suffer, both in UK and overseas. The value of such events in raising awareness of abuse should not be underestimated.

Chapter seven

PTSD and bullying

There are at least thirty-four physical symptoms of stress which result from bullying. There are an even greater number of psychological symptoms associated with bullying.

Bullying is traditionally linked with school playgrounds and children. However, adult bullying, including bullying in the workplace, is a frighteningly common occurrence. Bullying has not previously been linked to Post Traumatic Stress Disorder but the two will be more closely linked in the future when more research is made public. The first edition of this book did not make a link but, in line with the new clinical definition of PTSD in 1994, that omission has now been corrected. Victims of serious bullying exhibit the symptoms of a person who has experienced a serious, threatening situation.

The principal symptoms of PTSD are hypervigilance, an exaggerated startle response, flashbacks, nightmares, poor concentration, impaired memory, sleep disturbance and joint pains. It has been suggested that the symptoms of PTSD are also exhibited by those people who are exposed to prolonged stress, which has been described as Complex Post Traumatic Stress Disorder. A classic example of a likely Complex PTSD victim is the pathologist who is constantly presented with the awful and traumatic results of accidents and crimes.

Bullying is often protracted (Field 1996). Victims of bullying, whether it is bullying in the school playground or bullying in the workplace, are often subjected to prolonged periods of stress by the bully.

Bullying in the school playground has been researched and explored and it is now accepted that most schools have their bullies. Much less is known about bullying in the workplace. However, a growing amount of research is producing evidence which suggests that bullying in the workplace is extremely common.

For many, each day at work means constant criticism, humiliation, isolation and exclusion. It might include having increased responsibility but having authority removed, information withheld and training denied. In an insecure workplace, inadequate people cling to their jobs by bullying others. The underlying purpose of bullying is to hide inadequacy.

Bullying causes psychiatric injury that is invisible to all around. The symptoms are often obscured and mistakenly diagnosed as symptoms of mental illness. Hypervigilance is misinterpreted as paranoia; irritability and hypersensitivity are seen as a negative attitude; panic attacks are misdiagnosed as "work phobia", and poor concentration and impaired memory are viewed as having "personal problems".

In the climate of fear encouraged by the bully, strong feelings of shame, embarrassment and guilt are propagated. This is how bullies (and most abusers) silence their victims.

Arlette:

Here I was, in a responsible job, respected by my students or so I thought, and yet I was being bullied. I tried to avoid that word for ages but there was no doubt about it.

I felt trapped. Part of me just wanted to give up and leave my job. At the same time a voice inside kept saying 'why the hell should I?' But what could I do about it? Who could help me?

I could feel myself going downhill fast. I wanted to avoid going to work. The trouble was I wanted to avoid doing everything. It couldn't go on. In sane moments I tried to reason with myself that I could deal with these people - these bullies. I was educated, I should know what to do. But it was never that easy when it came down to the wire, when we were face to face.

Take the criteria for the diagnosis of PTSD, and apply them to the victim of serious bullying. It is clear that bullying can be considered a traumatic event which may result in the victim suffering from Post Traumatic Stress Disorder. That is not to say that all victims of bullying will suffer from PTSD in the same way that not all victims of trauma suffer from PTSD.

Because of the prolonged nature of many instances of bullying, when discussing the traumatic consequences of acts of bullying, the terms PTSD and Complex PTSD should be interchangeable.

Further evidence that bullying should be considered as a traumatic event and the cause of PTSD can be found in the reaction of victims to various triggers which remind them of their trauma or bullying. Bullied victims are faced with these triggers or reminders in the same way as victims of other types of trauma. Examples of these triggers might be:

- the sound of a door slamming which formerly announced the approach of the bully
- an accent or raised voice similar to that of the bully
- certain words or phrases which the bully used frequently, "bully catch-phrases"
- an official-looking envelope arriving in the post. Part of the bully's strategy is often to bombard the victim with threats of disciplinary action which might be heralded by the arrival of such an envelope

These triggers may appear to be simple everyday events, but then so was the sound of masking tape being pulled off a roll, and that sound terrified Terry Waite when he returned home from his hostage ordeal. The triviality of a trigger should not be an excuse to underestimate the effect that trigger may have on a victim.

Indeed, bullies may be fully aware of these triggers, and play them to their advantage. The trigger is then used with increased regularity and becomes an instrument of control. The victim finds that they eventually become immobilised not only by the trigger, but by the thought of the trigger.

One of the most common symptoms of PTSD is hypervigilance. It is also one of the most common symptoms displayed by the victims of bullying. It stems from a combination of distrust, obsession, fear and anxiety. These states combine to form a feeling of "over-alertness" in victims. They are always tensed and ready for trouble. Nevertheless, trouble still manages to take them by surprise.

It would be possible to proceed through the list of symptoms of PTSD and apply them to victims of bullying but that task has been left to other books. Suffice to say that the link between bullying and PTSD has been established, and several victims of bullying in the workplace have been clinically diagnosed as suffering from Post Traumatic Stress Disorder. That diagnosis has been accepted by the courts. Even more research into the link may be required before many sceptics will accept this situation.

One of the most recent mediums for the bully to exploit is modern communication networks - the Internet and mobile phones. Text messaging on mobile phones provides a perfect opportunity for the bully to operate at home, school or in the workplace. This 21st Century bully uses the speed and directness of modern communications to target victims and follow them wherever they go.

There are texts which deal exclusively with bullying, and in particular there are two texts published by Success Unlimited which cover the subject extensively. It would be better for those particularly concerned about bullying to read those texts rather than try and abbreviate the information here.

Both books are published by Success Unlimited in Oxfordshire:-

Bully in Sight, by Tim Field. 1996. 358 pages.

Bullycide: death at playtime, by Neil Marr and Tim Field. 2001. 303 pages.

A full-scale survey into the effects of bullying was published recently, and reported in the Spring 2001 edition of Counselling at Work. This survey, by Helge Hoel and Cary Cooper, looks and the causes and consequences of bullying at work. The report concludes that over 10 percent of the working population will have been bullied in any six month period.

Chapter eight

PTSD and children

It is not only adults who suffer from Post Traumatic Stress Disorder. The condition does not discriminate according to age. Of the death toll at Aberfan, 80 per cent were schoolchildren, and the survivors were also largely schoolchildren. Following the Dunblane shooting, most of the attention of the media was focused on the way that children cope with trauma.

Aberfan is an important milestone in the study and understanding of disasters and how people can be affected by trauma. This was the first major disaster to be covered comprehensively by the medium of television. On Friday 21 October 1966 black and white television pictures of the school engulfed in a landslide were beamed into millions of homes throughout Britain. Instantly the name Aberfan was on everybody's lips. Few knew where it was, but that did not prevent them from being deeply shocked by what they saw.

Twenty-five years later, attention turned to Romania. Socially deprived, the country had placed all its eggs in one basket. Children were grouped together in institutions where they experienced 'concentration camp' style conditions in what were officially described as orphanages. As with Aberfan, pictures of this human disaster were screened in millions of households. This time the pictures were transmitted world-wide, in colour and with appalling vividness.

Children in the Third World were starving to death. Match stick limbs and bloated stomachs were almost impossible to comprehend. The pictures were there, however. The disaster was real. Children were suffering from, amongst other things, the effects of trauma.

Prior to Aberfan, children were unlikely to have witnessed the effects of any major traumas. Their learning had not included pictures which could shatter many dreams in an instant. They simply had no knowledge of this kind of suffering.

Children today are more worldly. They have read the books, seen the film clips and bought the fund-raising T-shirt or red nose. Every child now has a memory of what a traumatic event can do. Their life experiences have been vastly increased by the media coverage of life-threatening events. This awareness may have a spiralling effect. The more children see trauma on television, the greater their perception of what might happen in a potentially life-threatening situation. Their illusion of safety has been steadily eroded over recent years.

The victims of major disasters can be subdivided into a number of groups:

Primary: survivors
Secondary: partners/families
Tertiary: witnesses
Quaternary: emergency service personnel

All four groups are 'at risk' of suffering from Post Traumatic Stress Disorder. The first three groups will include children. It is important that children's needs should be treated on an equal footing. The old adage that "he is too young to understand" may have some grounding in fact, but to try and change the expression to "he is too young to be traumatised" would be foolish in the extreme.

Many of the survivors at Aberfan were children (Miller 1974). They had lost friends and classmates. Teachers and the headmistress had also been killed. Somehow they had to pick up the pieces and continue with life.

In 1966, Post Traumatic Stress Disorder had not been formally recognised. These children were officially suffering from shock. Fortunately the scale of the disaster had some benefits. The issues were not removed from the list of acceptable topics of conversation. Many of the villagers wanted to talk about the events of that day. The topic was discussed openly and regularly. This was, perhaps, the first modern-day example of group therapy for patients who had suffered similar experiences.

There were reminders of the event all around the Welsh valley. The large grave. The devastated school. A population of children with entire age groups missing. The truth had to be faced, and by facing it together the community successfully started to rebuild itself.

Ten years after Aberfan, and on the other side of the Atlantic, another group of schoolchildren were caught up in a traumatic event of a different kind. One hundred miles to the south-east of San Francisco lies the town of Chowchilla. On 15 July 1976, the school bus was hijacked and twenty-six children were kidnapped. The children (aged 5-14 years) disappeared for 27 hours. They were taken by three masked gunmen and transferred to a 'hole in the ground' which was a buried truck trailer. They were buried for 16 hours until two of the oldest and strongest boys managed to dig them out.

The children and their parents were bombarded by the media.

A meeting was arranged for the parents and children at a medical health centre. At the meeting an ill-advised physician predicted that, statistically, only one of the twenty-six children would be emotionally affected by the experience. As no parent was willing to admit that their child was that 'one' there was a time lag of almost six months before parents asked for help.

A trauma specialist offered limited crisis treatment to the parents of the Chowchilla children (Terr 1981, 1983). After talking with each child, she concluded that every child showed signs of the emotional effects of psychological trauma. They were not identical to the symptoms of adult PTSD, but they were significant. Long after the kidnapping, 'fear of further trauma' continued to operate as a force behind 'fears of the mundane'.

One of the Chowchilla children was Larry Park who was six years old at the time. Even twenty years after the incident he still remembers exactly what it felt like.

Larry:
There's been a lot of fears that I wouldn't have without the kidnapping. I had nightmares, I was petrified of the dark, and I always thought people were trying to get the better of me.

In almost a repeat of the Chowchilla incident, another school bus was hijacked on 26 March 1997 near Durban, South Africa. On this occasion sixteen schoolchildren and four teachers of the

David Landau preschool in Asherville were held hostage during a twenty-minute ride. They were held at gun-point throughout the journey. The motive for the hostage-taking was apparently robbery as the four teachers were stripped of their valuables. The bus eventually stopped beside a sugar plantation and all the hostages were allowed to run for cover. Many were lost for hours before police search-parties managed to find them. The children and their teachers had truly believed they were going to be shot. They were terrified by the ordeal. However, nobody suffered any physical injury during the incident and so it received very little media attention within a nation well used to acts of violence.

Fortunately, incidents involving large numbers of children such as Aberfan (UK), Chowchilla (USA), Dunblane (UK) and Asherville (SA) are extremely rare, but traumatic events in general are alarmingly frequent. Children are very often secondary or tertiary victims of PTSD, because another family member has been involved in a serious or life-threatening event, or because they have witnessed such an event. These categories of victims are frequently overlooked by the medical profession. The first stages of treatment for the primary victim may also provide opportunities for staff to make an initial evaluation of possible secondary and tertiary victims. Nursing staff in accident and emergency departments are particularly well placed to identify these potential victims.

In 1988 I was involved in the investigation of a fatal road accident in which two children were killed (Kinchin 1988, Kinchin & Brown 2001). Whilst playing in a quiet residential street the children were unaware of the dangerous proximity of a street-cleaning vehicle. The driver reversed into the two children, crushing them both.

Whilst pondering how I was to identify the two unfortunate playmates, I was aware of a teenage girl approaching the accident scene. She suddenly rushed forward and knelt beside the blanket which had been placed over the young bodies. Her movements were so quick that nobody reacted swiftly enough to stop her lifting a corner of the blanket. By the time she had been forcefully lifted away, she had inadvertently identified her brother and a cousin. Everyone around was deeply distressed by the incident and our hearts went out to this girl.

Six months later, I revisited the family and spoke to the girl's father. He still mourned the loss of this son, and explained that his wife and daughter could not bring themselves to talk to me. The girl was frightened of policemen. They were still deeply distressed by vivid flashbacks and nightmares about the accident scene. That one event occupied their thoughts for much of the day, even six months later. I did not have the courage to admit to them that the incident had also affected me greatly.

Children's responses to a traumatic event will depend upon a number of factors, such as age, cognitive level, understanding of the traumatic event, and their closeness to the event and the primary victim.

Following the tragic death of Princess Diana on 31 August 1997, many children were deeply distressed by the event and by the continuous media coverage of the road accident in Paris, and of the funeral the following Saturday. Children interviewed on television referred to her as "the Queen of Hearts" and cried openly for her. In many ways, it is still more acceptable for children to cry than it is for adults. Perhaps because of this, children who are secondary or tertiary victims of PTSD recover from traumatic events more quickly than adults. Society does not impose the same suppressive codes upon the emotions of young people.

In December 2000 the Radio Times ran an article about Millvina Dean. Millvina is the youngest survivor of the Titanic sinking. She was just nine weeks old when the ship went down in 1912 after striking an iceberg. Although too young to remember the actual incident, her father drowned and her mother was seriously affected by the tragedy. At the ripe old age of 88 she confesses that she is unable to watch the epic film "Titanic" when it was shown on BBC TV over Christmas 2000. She said that the panic scenes at the end of the film would cause her to wonder about her father and that would be too distressing. Even though she was only 64 days old on the date that the ship sank, it still holds a traumatic memory for her.

Characteristics of PTSD unique to children

1 Repetitive (perhaps aggressive) play containing themes about the traumatic event.
2 Loss of recently-acquired developmental skills.
3 Omen formation - a false belief in being able to predict future untoward events.
4 Regressive behaviour, returning to thumb-sucking, bed-wetting, baby talk.
5 Generalised fearfulness and separation anxiety. Clinging.
6 Not wanting to sleep alone, wanting to sleep with parents.
7 Worry about how parents have reacted to the trauma.

Many characteristics of Post Traumatic Stress Disorder are exhibited by children who are taken into local authority care, although the term PTSD is rarely, if ever, applied to them. The fact that PTSD symptoms are manifested in these children is not surprising. The reasons for the care order are often linked to sexual or physical abuse, and to emotional and physical neglect. For children, this type of abuse and neglect is extremely traumatic and perceived as life-threatening. It has recently been argued that such victims of prolonged abuse are suffering from PDSD (Prolonged Duress Stress Disorder) (Scott & Straddling 1992) otherwise known as Complex PTSD. It is quite possible that the number of child PTSD sufferers exceeds the number of adult PTSD sufferers.

My own observation of foster children given into the care of my family had identified many instances of hyperalertness, sleep disorders, eating problems, regressive behaviour, self-abuse, uncustomary behaviour patterns and chronic anxieties. Many very young children taken into care will regress to drinking from a bottle and/or thumb-sucking. Some three-year-old children will regress in their play to activities normally associated with children a year younger. With careful planning, and plenty of tender loving care, this developmental lost ground can be speedily regained.

Every victim deserves good medical attention which should include help for any physical injuries, and possibly psychological counselling. Hospitals and accident departments can be intimidating places for adults. This is even more true for children. Even though the medical staff are well-intentioned, some of their routine procedures and detailed history-taking can feel like a second episode of the trauma. When children first arrive at the hospital, a loved one should be permitted to stay with them at all times (including during x-ray procedures). A child victim will be feeling vulnerable and a family member or friend can be briefed to give tactful reminders when medical staff probe too deeply, too quickly.

Trust is especially important if a victim is to discuss the traumatic event. When a child victim does decide to disclose what has happened and to share the nature of the trauma, the trustee must never react with disbelief or belittling comments. Neither must the victim be treated patronisingly.

Talking about trauma is vitally important and should be considered part of the medical care - not something staff enter into when there are slack moments.

Felicity:

It took me several weeks to build up towards telling someone about my brother. A couple of times I started to say something - but I got frightened that people would not believe me. Then I started to worry that I would be blamed. In the end, it was all too much and the truth burst out while I was having tea at a friend's house. Her parents were such understanding listeners. There were no awkward questions.

Simple and honest sharing of information will help the child to cope (Kinchin & Brown 2001), and will decrease any distorted perceptions of what has happened. However, it is NOT useful to make light of the event. If the event is perceived to be traumatic by the child involved - then traumatic it is.

The final task for medical staff is to provide guidance to the family concerning the child's possible reactions in the weeks and months following the traumatic event. A few minutes discussing the possible effects of the event will ease the worry when PTSD characteristics are identified.

CHILDREN AS SECONDARY VICTIMS

Children of today are almost as worldly as their parents. They fully understand how dangerous some situations may be and are just as likely to suffer from Post Traumatic Stress Disorder as any adult. I am convinced that, because of my assault my children were traumatised, and my actions towards my children were affected by my trauma. I would like to share one example of this.

David:

During the early summer of 1991 my daughter (aged 7 by this time) was expected to sit SATs (Standard Attainment Tests) at school. She was one of the first groups of children in the country to sit the tests which are now commonplace for all seven-year-olds. My wife and I decided that it was not appropriate for her to do this as it would add extra stress and trauma to her life. In consequence, she had to be withdrawn from school for a whole half term, and be taught by my wife and me. We were visited on a number of occasions by education officers from the LEA, and observed from a distance by the whole community.

Was the decision to withdraw our daughter from the SATs a sensible decision based on sound educational theory, or was it an emotional response to the traumatic environment of home - an attempt to protect our daughter from further trauma? Nobody will ever know the answer, but I often wonder whether we would have made the same choices had I not been so seriously attacked some nine months before the SATs began. Was I being over-protective towards my children? With hindsight, I think I was.

Had my daughter sat the tests the government had deemed fit for her, would the effects of the trauma, which had so seriously affected her quality of life, be taken into consideration? Had she been that much older and sitting GCSE examinations would any allowance have been made for the trauma she had experienced?

As I write this, all three of my children have now completed their compulsory education and all three have obtained above average results in their GCSE examinations. This was despite the traumatic incident which occurred to me all those years ago, and which affected them so deeply.

Even after all this time however, they still occasionally ask about my attack. It is not a taboo subject, and never has been.

Clearly, my children are not the only children to become secondary victims of PTSD. There are many such children. Most survive without any help or specialised treatment - at least we all hope they do!

Chapter nine

PTSD and terrorism

Terrorism undoubtedly causes people to suffer from Post Traumatic Stress Disorder. One of the most traumatic terrorist attacks of all time was the destruction of PanAm Flight 103 over Lockerbie on 21 December 1988. Jim Swire lost his daughter Flora (aged 24) in this act of terrorism. Jim became a household name as he championed the cause of justice in this case, following it to its conclusion in a Scottish Court, based in Holland, where a verdict of 'guilty' was passed on the bombers on 31 January 2001. The verdict came 4425 days after the bombing of the plane. However, in the United Kingdom the majority of terrorist incidents in the recent past have been linked to the political troubles in Northern Ireland.

On two occasions, I was privileged to listen to a presentation given by Aileen Quinton. Aileen's mother was murdered by the IRA at the Poppy Day Massacre in Enniskillen (Inniskilling) in 1987. Eleven people died immediately after the event. The twelfth victim, Ronnie Hill, died thirteen years later - having never regained consciousness. Ronnie was nursed by his wife Noreen. He was the much-appreciated principal of Enniskillen High School.

As a result of her personal experience, Aileen Quinton was an ardent campaigner in an attempt to raise awareness of the needs of trauma victims. The memory of this terrible massacre is now over thirteen years old but for many the images are still vivid.

Aileen ended her talks by presenting those in the audience with a 'handout' containing her ideas for treating trauma victims. She asked that these ideas be shared with as many people as possible. The more people who understand trauma the better the victim's life will be. Amongst the other pieces of information are a list of dos and don'ts for those who face the victims.

Eight Dos ...

- acknowledge the victim's experience.
- take your cue from the victim and help him find his own way.
- listen for as long as you can and reassure her that she does not have to protect you from her pain.
- accept the victim's feelings as they are and not just what you think they should be.
- accept the victim's tears (and your own) and avoid making him feel ashamed of crying in front of you.
- respect any need the victim has to seek information and make decisions relating to the incident or its aftermath. It is perfectly possible for a victim to be unable to sort out a phone bill, yet be capable of knowing, for example, that he must visit the site, or view the body. Everyday tasks may not be absolutely necessary for emotional survival which may explain why they are harder to complete.
- answer questions about the incident honestly.
- remember the children. Even the young suffer from traumatic events, however quickly they learn to hide this from adults, especially parents.

Eight Don'ts ...

- trivialise the victim's experience.
- resort to old clichés like "life goes on", "time will heal", "look to the future", "you've got to get on with the rest of your life". They do not help and can do a lot of harm by dismissing the significance of the victim's present feelings.
- force a victim to talk about trivia when she clearly wants to talk about what has happened to her. If you do it can add to the torture.
- make decisions on his behalf without consultation.
- associate not crying and bottling up feelings with bravery.
- feel that you have to do something spectacular or say something profound. Although giving someone an understanding and uncritical ear when she needs it may

not seem to you to be enough, if this is what you are doing then be assured you are worth your weight in gold.

- become embarrassed when the victim cries. Live with this slight discomfort.
- rush in with advice unless specifically asked. This is extremely hard to avoid but you could do a lot more harm than good.

Aileen also issues a smaller list of dos and don'ts for the victims themselves.

Do - claim the right to have and express your own feelings.

Do - allow yourself to cry. It can be painful, but is very therapeutic.

Do - take every opportunity to talk if you need to.

Do - remember that it is your situation that is abnormal and not you.

Do - make contact with others in a similar situation. You may be amazed and greatly relieved at how similar their feelings are. (Remember the trauma bond.)

Do - seek professional help if it all gets too much.

Do - allow yourself to progress in your own way at your own pace, staying still or going backwards if you need to. (Remember the snakes and ladders board.)

Do - take one day at a time.

Do not - let the way you perceive others to be coping add to your guilt.

Do not - push yourself too far too quickly in an effort to please others.

For almost a quarter of a century the media in Britain has shown an interest in the incident known as "The Birmingham Pub Bombings" which occurred on 21 November 1974 (Plimmer 1997). Much of this attention was devoted to the group of men called the "Birmingham Six" who were accused of planting the bombs that caused so much death and injury. But what of the true victims of that bombing campaign? I obtained this description of the incident from a man who had held this memory for over twenty-five years. Even after all that time, the details of the event are still clear to him.

Craig's is not one of the stories described in the chapters of this book but I feel that his memory of this traumatic event is worthy of sharing - word for word.

Craig:

"I remember it as if it were yesterday. I was just about to enter when there was a loud explosion from somewhere up the Street, I later discovered it was the pub in the Rotunda - The Mulberry Bush I think. I stopped and looked round when the bomb in the Tavern in the Town went off. The pub was below street level and I was about to enter the passage down to it. If the Rotunda bomb had not gone off first I doubt that I would be writing this now as I would have taken the full force of the blast escaping from the only available exit.

After a few seconds people started crashing out through the entrance and what I think was the barrel shoot. It may have been a fire exit. The first wave were blackened and extremely violent. They set about attacking litter bins, cars, anything within in reach. It was as if the gates of Hell had opened. I retreated to the hotel I was staying in on the other side of the street and watched from a window on the first floor directly opposite the pub doorway. The emergency services were there within minutes and started bringing up the injured. A nail bomb is pretty messy.

Then they brought up the dead on stretchers and improvised stretchers such as doors and the like. I could not understand why the injured were in such a mess while some of the dead had had all their clothes blown off them but otherwise looked untouched. (I read later that it was the nodes of the shock waves caused by the explosion in what was effectively a non-expandable box that caused this.)

A couple of firemen brought up bloody limbs and other body parts which were packed into black plastic sacks. I have this image of a fireman carrying a severed arm by the wrist as if it belonged to a mannequin.

Some time later the TV crew turned up and filmed the nearby shops damaged by the blast because the immediate scene in front of the pub was too horrific. Much later the street was closed and the army bomb disposal team turned up, I think to check for further devices. A record shop next door to the pub had a window display of Queen's Sheer Heart Attack album which depicted a photo of the group behind broken glass. It struck me that the broken glass of the shop window strewn about over crumpled posters of the group mimicked the record cover.

That's how it was. For several months I could not sleep properly as I kept dreaming that I had gone into the pub rather than stayed outside and the blast (in my dreams) kept waking me up. I became mildly claustrophobic and I still find it uncomfortable going into any building that has a similar entrance to that pub. Although I was not aware of it, I was accused of being morose, withdrawn and introspective throughout the following Christmas period. (Perhaps I am naturally like that at Christmas!) The whole episode is never far away even after all this time. I sometimes wonder whether the fireman carrying the severed arm thinks about it."

There must be thousands of people, like Craig, who have carried memories of traumatic events around with them wherever they go. Like unwanted baggage, these memories continue to travel with them until they can find some way of taking control of this memory. For some people it is possible for them to cope with this on their own. For others it may be necessary to seek out professional help - maybe years after the traumatic event.

For those who have struggled to contain such a memory for many years I recommend a detailed study of the dos and don'ts advocated by Aileen Quinton, who was a fellow sufferer.

I have specifically mentioned the names of Aileen Quinton, and Jim Swire, and Ronnie Hill and his wife Noreen, to draw attention to the fact that these acts affect the lives of many people for a very long time. Long after the media have forgotten the names, families are left struggling with the invisible injury and the hurt that such action brings.

Chapter ten

People who can help

It is unlikely that anyone can make a full recovery from Post Traumatic Stress Disorder on their own. They will require help from various sources. The longer they try to cope without help, the longer the condition is likely to persist.

PTSD is a state of mind. It is not possible for victims to control the symptoms until they are explained in a rational and acceptable fashion. The term 'mental illness' conjures up all manner of unpleasant images for many people, but it is often the term linked to PTSD. Because of this, I prefer to call PTSD an emotional condition (Turnbull 1993). Some people call PTSD a psychiatric injury. However, this labelling is something which the victim has to come to terms with - and this is not easy within a society that is generally afraid of the label 'mentally ill'.

Help for PTSD sufferers comes in many guises and from a variety of different occupations.

Sources of help for PTSD sufferers

Family doctors   PsychologistsCounsellors
Psychiatrists   Physiotherapists Support groups
Hospitals and convalescent homes Chiropractors
Independent help groups   Religious groups
Natural health practitioners Help and advice lines

WHEN DO YOU NEED HELP?

PTSD cannot be formally diagnosed until one month has gone by since the episode which triggered the disorder. However, immediately after the trauma, victims may experience disturbing symptoms and that is a normal reaction. In fact, if the symptoms of Post Trauma Stress are treated as they occur, the likelihood of developing Post Traumatic Stress Disorder is reduced.

There are nine situations which should indicate to you that it is time to seek help for PTSD:

1 If you continue to have nightmares and a poor pattern of sleep.

2 If you feel you cannot handle intense feelings or body sensations. If you feel that your emotions are not falling into place over a period of time. If you feel chronic tension, confusion, emptiness or exhaustion.

3 If after a month you continue to feel numb and empty. If you have to keep active in order not to feel this way.

4 If you have no person or group with whom to share your emotions and you feel the need to do so.

5 If your relationships seem to suffer badly, or if sexual problems develop.

6 If you have accidents through lack of concentration.

7 If you smoke, drink or take drugs to excess since the event.

8 If your work performance suffers.

9 If, as a helper, you are suffering from 'exhaustion'.

The month after a traumatic event is a period when you must be extra careful in everything you do. It is a time when you are at greater risk of having a road accident because you are in an upset state and probably less able to concentrate on what you are doing. It is also a time when accidents in the home are more likely to occur. Take extra care in the kitchen when preparing food, and take care when using any household appliances. With household chores, do not take any short-cuts which could prove dangerous.

Probably the first person who discusses the issue of help with you is a close relative, friend or colleague. It may be that you ask for their advice on the matter. Should you seek help? If you are asking the advice of friends, then why not go that one step further and seek the advice of a professional? In many instances, the first person you turn to is your family doctor. This is a logical step and I have no doubt you will be given a sympathetic hearing. Do not make light of your troubles. If they are serious enough for you to be considering discussing them with a professional, then they are serious enough for him or her to take notice. In the event of your GP not being sympathetic, you may wish to consider changing to another GP.

Perhaps the first task you will be asked to do is to complete some form of questionnaire to establish the scale of the event you experienced. There are many standard tests used to assess this. Some have been adapted and tailored to suit specific events which have affected many people. Others are of a standard type that could be applied to a variety of situations. They are nothing to be frightened of. The tests are simply a method of gauging a person's emotional state at any particular time. Some practitioners like to give these tests to their patients at regular intervals to measure any progress which may have taken place.

There are many types and styles of test. None should prove difficult and it is not a question of passing or failing. By asking a series of basic questions and grading your reply the test is simply a tool to assist with the best possible diagnosis of your condition. Some questionnaires take a different form. They may appear as a simple check list, or as an assessment of your mood. All test results, like any other part of your treatment, will be treated in the strictest confidence.

The most common type of test is the Beck Inventory or the Impact of Events test. Others may include a Fear Questionnaire, a work and social adjustment screening checklist, or a general health checklist. The work and social screening test is simply a way of establishing what is bothering you - it is your view of what is wrong at the present time. By working through the five headings, you gauge your ability to cope with particular things. For question one, if you are coping quite well at work then you might perhaps award yourself a score of one. If work is intolerable then you might score seven or even eight.

Many family doctors will be unfamiliar with Post Traumatic Stress Disorder. They may have seen only a handful of cases and be unsure what treatment to offer. Consequently they will wish to refer your case to somebody with more expertise in the field. This is no criticism of family doctors. They follow similar procedures when they deal with many other ailments. Accept such a referral in good faith.

Some trauma victims are first admitted to hospital because of physical injuries. Victims of large-scale events can be processed in what appears to be an impersonal manner. Some hospitals operate a system of numbering casualties and constantly referring to them by that number. This is not a deliberate attempt to distress and dehumanise victims - it simply makes the quick processing of large numbers of casualties easier to administer.

Early symptoms of Post Traumatic Stress can show soon after the incident. Some symptoms may be present whilst the victim is still in the Accident and Emergency Department of the hospital. In some instances the symptoms may manifest themselves when the victim is transferred to a ward.

David:

The crowd closed in on me. I could just see a sea of faces. I hit out hard, and tried to move away. Hands grabbed at my arms and somebody sat across my legs. Then I could hear somebody calling my name.

I felt a little dizzy as I looked about me and realised I was surrounded by nursing staff. I was fighting with the nursing staff!

The hospital should be prepared for such reactions if they know they are dealing with the victims of traumas. The trouble is, the hospital staff may not know you have suffered a serious, potentially life-threatening event. To busy casualty staff you are just another case.

Richard:

A colleague came into the hospital to take my statement. He kept on and on about the guy who had started the fire. He went into great detail about how the fire had started and how badly injured the rest of the family were.

I was shaking badly and spent most of the time jumping whenever a door closed or somebody dropped something. I couldn't concentrate on the statement. I didn't want to talk about the fire.

Occasionally, the slightest thing can be a trigger which sets off a series of events in the mind of the victim.

Cindy:

They kept me in hospital overnight because I had been knocked out. They said I was suffering from concussion. My head was still ringing from the blow I had received from the ladder. I was tucked up in bed, and they settled me down for the night.

I eventually fell asleep.

There was a loud metallic crash. Somebody had dropped something near my bed. Instantly, I was awake and I could picture the building site. I could hear the sounds of men at work and I wanted to get away from it all. I jumped out of bed and ran. I was convinced I was in danger if I remained where I was. I tried to 'hide' in a corner of the corridor. It must have looked really funny. Two nurses came after me and stopped a few yards from where I crouched.

Nobody said anything. The nurses just didn't know what had happened to me. I stood up, slowly. I was in hospital, not by the building site. I could feel the tears. Why had I run away like that?

What was wrong with me?

It is normal to be disorientated following a traumatic event. The body is in shock and the chemical messages being triggered by the brain are causing internal confusion amongst the senses. It might feel strange, or frightening. Victims might think they are acting abnormally and that they are out of control. This is not the case.

During the traumatic event, the protective mechanisms of the body were overloaded, passing messages and trying to predict dangers. As you were experiencing an abnormal situation, the body did not know what to expect and so tried to prepare for everything. Having set your body this impossible task it should be no surprise that it is going to take time for your body chemistry to readjust to the safety in which you now find yourself. This is normal.

Hospital staff should be aware of this and act accordingly. You should be given time to talk and explain why you are so distressed. Explain why you thought you were in danger. What did you think was going to happen to you?

In one respect, those who experience a large-scale traumatic event have an advantage. They will be amongst other victims who experienced the same event, and those who are caring for them will anticipate some of the symptoms of Post Trauma Stress. Those people who experience more isolated traumatic incidents do not have this dubious advantage. Their carers will have no idea that they have suffered a serious and potentially life-threatening event.

Felicity:

My friend's parents suggested that I go and see my doctor. I couldn't really understand why! I was not ill or sick, so why see a doctor?

In the end I did go. The doctor was great. She simply sat and listened to my story. She did not examine me. There were no difficult questions. At the end of my appointment she did not even give me a prescription. It was not like any other doctor's appointment I have had. Yet I felt so much better afterwards.

Attending hospital or seeing your family doctor is usually the first step towards obtaining help and relief from the symptoms of Post Traumatic Stress Disorder. This is the starting point for most sufferers.

Thereafter, there are numerous courses of treatment open to sufferers. Don't be dismissive of anything you are offered. Keep an open mind on most treatments and assess the merits of each one. Treatments can be divided into two groups:

1 Those that treat the intrusive and avoidant symptoms.

2 Those that treat the physical symptoms of PTSD.

Psychiatrists, psychologists, counsellors, religious groups and self-help groups tend to concentrate on treating the intrusive and avoidant symptoms, while physiotherapists, chiropractors and natural health practitioners deal with the physical symptoms of the condition. It is usually the job of the family doctor to liaise and mediate between all these specialists and to have an overview of your treatment. Everything should be reported back to your doctor so that he may co-ordinate your recovery.

Reminder of the symptoms of PTSD
INTRUSIVE - Recurrent and distressing recollections.
- Flashbacks, thoughts, nightmares, dreams.
- Phobias about specific daily routines, events or objects.
- Feelings of guilt for having survived.
AVOIDANT - Detachment from others, emotional numbness.
- Avoidance of thoughts or feelings associated with the event.
- Markedly diminished interest or pleasure in most activities.
PHYSICAL - Sleep problems.
- Hypervigilance.
- Exaggerated startle response.
- Joint/muscle pains.
- Feelings of nervousness.
SOCIAL - Violent outbursts.
- Increased irritability.
- Impaired memory.
- Inability to concentrate.
- Irrational or impulsive behaviour.
- Low self-esteem.

Clearly by treating some intrusive symptoms the effect of physical symptoms will also be lessened. Indeed, treating any symptom will help overall. The simplest way to look at the methods of treatment is to examine them according to what they set out to achieve.

TREATMENT OF INTRUSIVE AND AVOIDANT SYMPTOMS
Recent studies of the role of neurotransmitters in the victim's brain have resulted in exciting advances in modern medicine. There is probably a simple chemical explanation for Post Traumatic Stress Disorder, but at present this can only be guessed at. What is certain is that the chemical messages transmitted by the brain during times of crisis can be overstretched in some way. The messages have become confused and there are too many of them. To treat the intrusive and avoidant symptoms of PTSD is to rectify and steady the flow of these chemical messages.

The chemical messengers which are of particular importance are the neurotransmitters known as noradrenaline and adrenaline, (called norepinephrine and epinephrine in America) endorphins and serotonin. The noradrenaline alerts the brain to the crisis. The endorphins help us to calm down and deal with the crisis while at the same time acting as a painkiller. During severe stress, serotonin is depleted and the reason for this is unclear. It is believed that the decrease of these neurotransmitters following a traumatic event leads a traumatised person to feel depressed. The depression experienced by victims of PTSD is chemically different from depression in non-traumatised persons.

Many PTSD symptoms are brought about by faulty chemical messages being transmitted within the body. Prescribed drugs can be administered to rectify these chemical imbalances but this is a short-term treatment. The long-term solution is to 'talk it out', and become so at ease with discussing the trauma that the chemical messages of panic are no longer triggered. This is a job for an expert. Trauma counsellors, psychiatrists and psychologists are all trained to help victims control these triggers. It is often a slow process but it is the long-term treatment to cure PTSD.

TREATMENT OF PHYSICAL AND SOCIAL SYMPTOMS
The aches and pains linked to any stress can be severe. Those linked to PTSD can be simply awful. Limbs can be so tense that the pain in muscles becomes unbearable. Backache and headaches can also dominate daily existence.

Sleeplessness, irritability, poor memory, outbursts of violence and other physical symptoms can all be linked to the way we feel. There are several ways of relieving these symptoms. Some involve conventional treatments while others resort to natural remedies. All of them have been found to help ease the situation.

To be able to take full advantage of any counselling you must be able to relax. When your body is very tense, relaxing becomes almost impossible. Well-meaning people telling you to relax just make matters worse. Your body will need help to relax it and that help can take a variety of forms.

Physiotherapy is most often linked to aiding recovery from physical injuries. To attend a physiotherapist with an 'invisible' or psychological injury may appear rather odd. Indeed, a few physiotherapists may turn you away. Fortunately most will admit you to their clinic and, as soon as they feel how tense your body has become, they will appreciate your need for treatment.

The same can be said for chiropractors. The tensions and aches caused by PTSD can be soothed and eased considerably by the attentions of a qualified chiropractor.

There are a variety of natural health practitioners who can help victims learn how to relax. Best known are aromatherapists and practitioners of reflexology, and other massage techniques such as shiatsu.

It is one of the paradoxes of the 1990s that in this high-tech age the wonderful healing properties of essential oils, herbs, massage and simple relaxation techniques are being reintroduced to the complex world of healthcare.

It would be difficult to describe every treatment for PTSD in one book. However, it is necessary to explain a variety of different treatments and to show how they have been found to work effectively. Each victim will respond differently to treatment. Some treatments will be found wanting in some instances. Don't let the failure of one course of treatment discourage you from trying something different. Remember the snakes and ladders board.

Whatever treatments you choose to follow, remember the importance of having one person overseeing your total treatment. With such an arsenal available to combat the symptoms of PTSD it is necessary to have one person to marshal these treatments into some logical progression. Counselling must be combined with relaxation techniques. Medication may be required at various stages of your recovery to help overcome the feelings of depression, frustration and anxiety. The one person best placed to oversee all of these treatments is your family doctor.

The next chapter examines some methods of treatment which have been found to succeed in the eleven cases which are highlighted in this book.

Chapter eleven

Treatments for PTSD

DRUG THERAPY

There are many drugs that can help PTSD victims on the road to recovery. The list includes:

1 Antidepressants
   a) tricyclic antidepressants (TCAs)
   b) monoamine oxidase inhibitors (MAOIs)
   c) serotonin re-uptake inhibitors (SSRIs)
2 Hypnotics (sleeping tablets)
3 Beta-adrenoceptor blockers (beta-blockers)
4 Analgesics (painkillers)

In many cases of Post Traumatic Stress the chemical imbalance within the body has been badly disturbed. These prescribed drugs help that balance return to normal.

Look upon medication as a way of starting your course of treatment. Following a traumatic, potentially life-threatening event the body is in chaos. It takes some time for the brain to accept that the danger has passed. Physically, your body is exhausted and needs a rest. The medication is a good way of resting the body so that it is fit to make a recovery from the trauma.

Medication can help reduce pain and shaking, ease sleeping and aid relaxation. Tablets will not do the whole job for you, but they will help considerably by reducing anxiety levels. Medication should often be considered as the first step towards recovery.

However, if you are anxious about taking the medication this action may be counter-productive. Discuss the possible options with your doctor. Be guided by him/her, but make the final decision yourself. Discuss the possible side-effects of taking some of these drugs. Remember that most of the new generation drugs have very mild side effects. Find out how long you are likely to be needing the drug. The length of some courses of treatment may seem daunting to some sufferers, but some of these drugs do not even begin to work effectively until they have been taken regularly for several weeks.

It is worthwhile taking a brief look at each of the four main groups of drugs available to PTSD sufferers.

1. Antidepressants

These drugs are not only administered to people who have a classic case of depression. Depression often exists alongside PTSD and it is right that that depression should be treated. Using antidepressant drugs is one way of treating depression in traumatised people. Antidepressants can also be used to treat loss of appetite, sleep disturbances and panic disorders.

There are several groups of antidepressant drug. Most common are the tricyclic drugs which are the original antidepressants and include amitriptyline and imipramine. Should these prove unsuccessful patients may be prescribed monoamine oxidase inhibitors (MAOIs) such as phenelzine and isocarboxazid. However, patients taking MAOI antidepressants have to maintain strict control of their diet. They cannot eat cheese, pickled herring or broad bean pods. Neither should they drink any beverages containing meat or yeast extract like Bovril, Vegemite, Oxo or Marmite.

There are other drugs which have antidepressant properties, and the one which PTSD victims are most likely to be prescribed is a drug which inhibits the uptake of serotonin in the body, called fluoxetine hydrochloride (Prozac). Prozac had a bad press some time ago, but it is one of the best drugs for treating serious cases of PTSD (Busuttil 2001) and it is now much cheaper to prescribe.

Alcohol should be avoided by all patients taking antidepressants. The drugs exaggerate the effect of alcohol on the brain. They may make you drunk very quickly.

Many drugs have side-effects and antidepressants are no exception to this. A good doctor will explain the possible side-effects which might be experienced. There is no way of predicting which patients will be adversely affected by which drugs. Most antidepressants must be taken, as prescribed, for at least three weeks before any benefits of the drug can be appreciated.

Christine:

I couldn't sleep. I couldn't eat. I didn't want to do anything. I was sick inside. Eventually, I agreed to take some pills but I just took one or two and they didn't seem to work. Then my doctor gave me a good talking to. He explained that there was no magic overnight cure. It wasn't a case of take one of these and it will cheer you up. I then started to take the pills properly. After about four weeks I felt considerably better. I suffered from a dry mouth and so drank lots of fruit juice but that was much better than feeling so depressed.

Views on the quantity of the drug prescribed vary significantly. In the case of amitriptyline many physicians recommend 125mg or 150mg daily as being a good therapeutic dose. However, many patients cannot tolerate more than 85mg without the quality of their life being adversely affected. Dose levels can easily be adjusted to suit individual needs.

David:

At first I was given one antidepressant for a few weeks. The side effects were awful. I felt drunk and couldn't wake up properly. I had a headache nearly all the time.

So I was changed to another drug. That worked well for a couple of months but then I began to experience side-effects from that drug too.

Finally, after several other failures, I was given fluoxetine hydrochloride (Prozac). There were no side-effects despite taking it for many months.

Withdrawal from antidepressants should be gradual. In many cases complete withdrawal takes one or two months.

2. Hypnotics

Sleep is a problem for many PTSD sufferers. In the short term it is sometimes necessary to prescribe drugs which help regulate a pattern of sleep. Such drugs are normally prescribed over a short period of time at stages in recovery where victims are near exhaustion due to lack of sleep.

Paul:

I just needed something to help me sleep. I would lie awake for hours worrying about all kinds of things. Then, when I did get off to sleep I would wake up at about three o'clock in the morning and that would be the end of the night as far as I was concerned.

My doctor gave me some sleeping tablets, just enough to last me for three weeks. That saw me over a bad patch and although I didn't sleep for very long when I came off the drugs, my quality of sleep had improved.

Drugs such as loprazolam and temazepam act for a short time and they have little or no hangover effect the following morning. There are some problems with withdrawal from these 'hypnotics' in a few cases.

3. Beta-adrenoceptor blockers

Beta-blockers do work well for some PTSD victims. They reduce symptoms such as palpitations, sweating and shaking and so reduce the worry and fear that these symptoms produce.

Although they were not originally intended for this treatment, beta-blockers relieve the symptoms of hypertension and anxiety and are very useful in reducing the effects of panic experienced by some PTSD sufferers.

4. Analgesics

Many PTSD victims suffer with pain brought about by physical injuries and other pains brought on by tension, stress and cramp. On occasions these pains can become severe. Preparations such as aspirin, paracetamol and codeine can be purchased without prescription and many PTSD sufferers administer their own analgesics to relieve pain. However, on some occasions the pain may be so strong that a prescribed medication is required.

In any event, sufferers who are already taking drugs prescribed by their doctor should check with their doctor or pharmacist before self-administering any painkillers. Not all drugs mix with one another and it is as well to check first.

When dealing with any drug which affects the central nervous system care should be taken and professional advice sought.

Some of the side-effects of certain drugs are the same as the symptoms of PTSD. Consequently, these side-effects become difficult to recognise for what they are (Hammersley 1992). It should be stressed that whilst some people never experience any side-effects, the chances of them occurring increase with long-term use.

Some of the unwanted side-effects of medication are:- nausea, headache, vomiting, blurred vision, constipation, tinnitus, diarrhoea, dizziness, vertigo, rashes, low blood pressure, lethargy, impotence, loss of libido, numbness, psychological anxiety, poor concentration, confusion, agoraphobia, panic attacks, irritability, tension, obsessions, social withdrawal, depression, poor memory, aggressive outbursts.

PSYCHOTHERAPY

Some people avoid the term 'psychotherapy'. It simply means the treatment of nervous disorders by psychological methods. This type of therapy is practised by psychiatrists, psychologists and the counsellors employed by various help groups. Psychotherapy can help to reduce the effect of the intrusive and avoidant symptoms experienced by PTSD sufferers.

Within the field of psychotherapy there exists a large variety of approaches to the treatment to PTSD. It is impractical to explain them all, but the most common forms of therapy are counselling, real-life exposure and imaginal exposure.

Counselling involves sitting down and talking to someone - someone whom you can trust. This may be a close friend or relative, or it may be a professional counsellor working within the health service or for a voluntary group or organisation. Some employers also provide counsellors to care for the psychological needs of their work force.

Victims of trauma often have a negative view. Those who go on to develop PTSD will regularly have a low expectation of life and will often become depressed as a result. The job of a counsellor is not to change the negative thoughts and feelings into positive ones, but to turn them into realistic ones.

A textbook counselling session will be divided into three parts. The digging into the trauma, or 'dirty work', will be done during the first third of the session. Any exploration of that 'digging' will be carried out during the middle session, leaving the final third of the counselling session to settle and calm the client. That is the 'rule of thirds' theory (Kluft 1989).

With PTSD sufferers the drop-out rate from counselling sessions is high: higher that the drop-out rate for clients suffering with depression or anxiety. This being the case, counsellors are under pressure to relax PTSD victims and not to alienate them. How this is achieved is up to the individual counsellor.

Consequently a typical PTSD counselling session might start by enquiring into the sufferer's current state; a look at the high points and low points in the last few days. This might be followed by a review of the previous session's homework. (Yes, counsellors give homework assignments!) The session may then move into a period of 'dirty work'. This may well lead into the setting of more homework and conclude with any feedback on the day's session.

This example does not strictly follow the 'rule of thirds', but in the real world of counselling it is not always possible to stick with theoretical models.

Any counsellor worthy of the title will be loyal and treat anything discussed during the session in the strictest confidence. It may take several meetings before a good client-counsellor link can be established. That is not unusual. For those sufferers who come from a macho background it will be hard to be honest about emotions and feelings. However, honesty is what is required if the sessions are to have any benefit.

Clearly the first few meetings with your counsellor will be largely devoted to a description of the traumatic event which led you to feel that your life was under threat. For the sufferers who experienced one single incident this can be a straightforward narrative. For those who have suffered a repeated trauma, it is not practical to describe each incident as a separate issue. There may be too many and the memories of similar events will have blurred together. Usually, however, there are a few distinct and meaningful incidents which have remained freshest in the memory.

Some PTSD sufferers will be unsure what has caused the disorder to manifest itself. They will be taken through various stages in their life by the counsellor in order to find the real trauma which has affected them so deeply.

Being counselled can be both distressing and exhausting. A one-hour counselling session can sap the physical strength of the strongest person. If this is happening the counsellor will sense this and slow down the rate at which counselling tasks are set for you. Using the snakes and ladders board image, it is worth reminding yourself that you may have to slide down one or two snakes before you find the correct route to the winning square at the top of the board.

Graham:

My wife is of the opinion that the PTSD was brought on by the counsellors at the convalescent home. I felt well and showed no sign of PTSD before attending them. Could the sessions have triggered it off?

It is most unlikely that a counsellor will induce PTSD in a client. However, a counsellor may bring the condition to the surface and expose feelings which have been submerged for some time. It may well feel that the counselling has made you worse instead of better. That belief will only be short-lived.

Jessica:

I couldn't work out what had happened to me. I used to be so happy-go-lucky but after the baby I started to worry so much. It was not until after she started school that I saw a counsellor and the subject of Post Traumatic Stress was mentioned. I took a bit of convincing at first, but eventually I became so relieved to find that what I was experiencing was 'normal'. My counsellor helped me to see this. He was very patient with me.

Sometimes we are frightened that people are going to laugh, or suggest that the trauma was caused by our own mismanagement of the situation. These thoughts can be a barrier to successful counselling and will have to be addressed at some point, sooner rather than later.

Felicity:

My probation officer suggested that I should see a counsellor. Eventually I agreed. When I first saw her I talked about drug taking and boys. I talked about my fear of the police and of my father's drinking and driving conviction. I made out that I had been around and knew a thing or two. Eventually all this silly talk dried up and I was quieter. Then one day I walked into a session and told her about my brother and what he had done. She did not show any shock. She did not say I was a worthless slut, or anything like that.

I realised that I trusted my counsellor. It was such a relief to me.

Good counselling is non-judgemental. Counsellors are not there to give moral lectures or to say that things could have been better if you done this, or done that. Counsellors will help you look at the trauma head-on and realise that you have coped remarkably well with this potentially life-threatening event. You are normal.

Counsellors often give their clients homework. Realistically, PTSD sufferers cannot hope to find the solution to their troubles during a weekly one-hour counselling session. There has to be more than that. Sufferers may be asked to keep a diary: writing briefly about what had happened, how they feel, what they are worried about. The diary is for nobody else to read, although it can be shared with the counsellor. The purpose of writing things down is to make them real. Writing about trauma is therapeutic in itself. It also provides a record of feelings and emotions so that when things look pretty low one can look back through the diary and realise that things were worse a few weeks ago.

Diaries also help you to keep track of time. If PTSD is preventing you from working then you will have plenty of time on your hands. Having a diary will encourage you to complete some chores and make a note of your successes and your failures. It will help to give some structure to each day.

Counsellors may ask you to make lists. These lists may form the basis of the next counselling session. A list might itemise the people you are angry with. It might be the tasks you have successfully completed in the last month. It could be a list of the times you have successfully conquered a fear or phobia.

Another task that might be set for you to complete is to write a 'fear script'. A fear script is simply a narrative of the traumatic event. Chapter 2 is a collection of fear scripts prepared by the eleven people who have volunteered their personal stories for this book.

The regular re-reading and re-writing of a fear script will, in time, make the event appear less traumatic to the writer. It is a way of placing events into a logical perspective.

CRISIS COUNSELLING

This is the term given to emergency counselling following a traumatic event. A crisis counsellor will usually only have one or two sessions with a sufferer with the aim of helping to establish that a trauma has taken place (Scott 1992). The crisis counsellor will have to help the sufferer answer vital questions:

Am I safe now?

What if I don't get better?

What is going to become of me?

What is or has been happening to me?

At the point of crisis the sufferer is too distressed and overwhelmed by events to begin any structured counselling course. The sufferer will need space to try to cope for themselves, but some gentle assistance with this coping may enhance the chances of swift recovery.

OTHER THERAPY

There are two other types of therapy likely to be offered to those who suffer with chronic PTSD: imaginal exposure and real-life exposure.

Imaginal exposure involves the sufferer imagining their trauma in great detail, using their own words. This should eventually be done in the first person, present tense, as if they were actually going through it all again. All five senses are used in imagining the trauma (Richards 1991).

This technique can be graded. This is done by using the least frightening of a number of images, or by using the third person, or past tense. Sessions should be audiotaped.

Some sufferers can become very distressed at the mere mention of any imaginal exposure procedure. (It terrified me!) The topic should not be explored in depth by the therapist until some level of trust and rapport has been established. Some sufferers are resistant to the idea of making a tape of their trauma. This can be the case even with the safeguard that the tape will only be used in the counselling sessions.

David:

It all went pear-shaped when she ended the counselling session with the words '. . . and then we will start the graded imaginal exposure therapy'. Those few words were enough to start me sweating.

Once a tape has been made it should be played regularly as 'homework'. Often sufferers will want to remake the tape because they have left out aspects of the trauma. Care must be taken to limit the length of the tape. Too much information can make the tape last too long, and the therapy is then in danger of becoming a heavy burden. Tapes should be restricted to a maximum of 30 minutes.

It should be stressed that the first week of using imaginal exposure is usually the worst. It is much like the effects felt by a heavy smoker who gives up the habit. They experience increased tension, irritability and disturbed sleep. These returning symptoms may lead the sufferer to question why they are bothering with the therapy, particularly if they were feeling much better at the onset. It is vital for the therapist to confront the sufferer's doubts and assist in explaining why they feel so bad. Failure to do this may lead to the sufferer abandoning the treatment in the early stages.

After two to three weeks the sufferer should become more comfortable with the therapy. Like the ex-smoker, there will still be some discomfort, but it will be more manageable.

Sufferers may also be encouraged to experience a graded real-life exposure to the trauma or to phobias which are triggers to flashbacks. Real-life exposure is exactly what it says. It is graded exposure to those things which provoke images of the trauma. This type of therapy is often offered to phobics and is now being offered to PTSD sufferers. However, there are some situations where real-life exposure is neither practical nor possible, and imaginal exposure will have to be used on its own.

Marlene:

The first stage of my real-life exposure was to take a ride in a cab. Simple really. It came around to my home address. My counsellor and I got in. We drove around the block and back to my home. The driver thought we were nuts. I spent most of my time with my eyes closed and concentrating on breathing in . . . 1 2 3 4 5 and then out again . . . 1 2 3 4 5 6. The trip lasted about four minutes.

This was an introduction to a real-life exposure treatment which was to last many weeks.

Marlene:

By the third week I was ready to go in the cab on my own. By this time I had told one or two of the drivers what I was up to. Instead of laughing at me, they took their role very seriously and were extremely supportive.

After my first 'solo' trip I was told by the driver, 'You did just great, lady,' and he actually reduced my fare.

The order in which imaginal exposure and real-life exposure is carried out must be discussed by the sufferer and therapist. There is no absolute rule about which should come first. However, it is generally felt that imaginal exposure should be started first. For reasons unknown, this exposure tends to help ease the depressive state of some PTSD sufferers and can improve their mood. Real-life exposure appears to be most effective with sufferers who are less depressed.

With all therapy of this type it is important to set targets and goals. In Marlene's case the goal was to feel comfortable when driven in a car by other people. She had been a passenger in both of the road accidents in which she was involved. Each week, Marlene set a target. 'By the end of this week, I shall have travelled in a cab for a 15-minute trip.' The targets were gradually extended until her goal was in sight.

Setting targets is important. There is also an element of risk attached to the practice. When targets are reached it feels marvellous. When you fail to reach targets it can be very depressing. Simple targets can sometimes appear unattainable.

Targets and goals must be set at realistic levels. What is realistic for a PTSD sufferer may appear ridiculously easy to anyone else - so what! Your targets must be achievable and worthwhile. Discuss your targets with your therapist.

Many PTSD sufferers complain that they are kept in the dark about their treatment. In the early stages this is probably quite reasonable. Life has become confused enough, and having some expert explaining theories of behaviour psychotherapy would be a waste of everybody's time.

However, as time goes by it becomes important for someone to explain what has happened to you and how the damage to your emotions can be rectified. Therapists should take time to explain what they are doing and what they want you to do. Giving reasons for courses of action is important. Giving reasons for courses of treatment is vital if the treatment is to be followed through to its conclusion.

PTSD sufferers as a group are often hesitant when it comes to seeking treatment for their condition. The issues of distrust and loss of dignity appear to be intense. This is most common amongst the victims of violence - slightly less common in victims of natural disasters. In cases of bullying, abuse and violation the sense of betrayal can be overwhelming. Treatment must have a high degree of acceptability to the victim. This acceptability is one of the main factors predicting a successful outcome.

Therapy offered by employers is often rejected by employees. This is particularly so amongst emergency service and armed service personnel. It appears to be largely a matter of trust. In particular, police officers are reluctant to trust counselling offered by the police service (Kinchin 1993). Many prefer to seek counselling from therapists with no direct link to the police. There is a fear that the confidentiality of the therapy is at risk if the counselled and the counsellor are employed by the same authority. This fear may be wholly unfounded in almost all cases, but that fact does not dispel the fear.

Medication appears to be helpful in conjunction with psychotherapy because decreasing the sufferer's distress can make it easier for him or her to focus on the traumatic memories.

Finally, a significant number of PTSD victims suffer from predominantly physical symptoms. Unless these symptoms are assessed carefully by a medically trained person and an adequate reason is given for their presence, these victims are likely to reject any psychological treatment. Treatment of the physical symptoms is important.

PHYSIOTHERAPY

Many PTSD sufferers experience physical symptoms of the disorder. These symptoms require some form of physical therapy to ease them. Such therapy can be obtained from a physiotherapist, a chiropractor or a natural health practitioner.

The term 'physiotherapy' simply means the treatment of an injury by physical means such as manipulation, massage or exercise rather than by the administration of drugs. There is no reason why physiotherapy should not work in harmony with drug therapy and psychotherapy. Moreover, there is no reason why physiotherapy should not be used to alleviate the physical symptoms of an emotional condition such as PTSD. Unfortunately, not all practitioners of physiotherapy have come to appreciate the value their treatment can have for a PTSD sufferer.

Professional massage is a good treatment at any time. For the sufferer of PTSD, massage can help to relax muscles which have become tense and rigid. Back and neck massage can relieve these symptoms admirably. Massage of the limbs is also of benefit. Physiotherapists can offer massage as part of a course of treatment. Chiropractors can also offer a similar treatment.

Exercise is important to everyone. Some victims of trauma may have physical injuries which require specific exercises. Those with no physical injuries can still benefit from a structured exercise regime designed to motivate them into positive thinking. Striving for improved physical fitness (even at a moderate level) can boost self-esteem and aid recovery.

Physiotherapists have a wide range of electrical and mechanical machinery to assist the body in recovering from injury. One piece of equipment of significance to PTSD sufferers is a micro-electronic exerciser which provides interferential therapy (DeDomenico 1982).

This method of treatment has been widely used for many years by the medical profession and is now being used to ease the symptoms of PTSD. So how does it work? Normally, during physical exercise your muscles are caused to contract by electrical impulses transmitted from your brain. The interferential therapy involves two medium frequency currents used to produce a low frequency effect. An 'interference effect', equal to the difference in frequency between the two currents, is produced. At a frequency of 100Hz this has an analgesic effect, while at a lower 20Hz the treatment relaxes the muscles. A straightforward, natural, and effective principle.

David:

I had not been sleeping very well since my assault. Then my physiotherapist suggested interferential. I was happy to try anything once. Two electrodes were placed at the bottom of my neck, and two more at the base of my spine. The machine was set at a very low frequency (20Hz) and I could feel a light tingling running up and down my back. The treatment lasted for 20 minutes. I fell asleep after just five.

By using very low frequency, intermittent alternating electrical currents, body tension and insomnia can be eased. The treatment will induce gentle relaxation of the body, soothing tension, easing muscular pain and creating a general feeling of well-being. Relaxation to aid sleep can be induced by the gentle, rhythmic pulses that are the essence of interferential treatment.

With interferential therapy there is no uncomfortable skin stimulation. It can be used as a treatment in its own right - but it is more commonly used in combination with other forms of treatment.

Paul:

I was so tense and worked up that the slightest noise made me jump violently. I found that interferential helped my body relax. Early on in my recovery it was the only treatment which enabled me to relax.

This treatment can be administered daily for 20-30 minutes. The results are amazing. Unfortunately, the treatment cannot be offered to pregnant women or anybody with a heart condition or with a pacemaker fitted.

The treatments described here are a sample of the various types of physiotherapy available to PTSD sufferers. New treatments are being added to this list every year.

RELAXATION

Time to relax is essential. Not just for PTSD sufferers but for everyone. The problem arises when people lose the ability to relax naturally. In an ideal world everyone would have a strategy to help himself relax following times of stress or crisis. Time should be set aside for relaxation.

It is sad that we do not live in an ideal world and many of us have lost the ability to relax our bodies. Consequently, those of us who have experienced a traumatic, potentially life-threatening event will have to find ways of helping to ease the tension that comes with PTSD. We have to learn how to relax.

Aromatherapy can form part of a healing regime as well as being a preventive therapy in its own right. It gives pleasure through the sense of touch (massage), the sense of smell (aromatic oils), the sense of sight (pleasant surroundings), and sometimes through the sense of hearing (soft music). By so doing, it helps to create favourable conditions in body and mind for healing to take place quite naturally.

It is not uncommon to find aromatherapy being used in hospitals as an aid to relaxation. Aromatic oils can be burned on special bedside burners, or mixed with a carrier oil and used in massage.

When using this therapy it is vital to find an aroma which you like. It is pointless to try to relax with a smell that you cannot tolerate. Perhaps the best natural oil for PTSD sufferers is neroli. This is distilled from the blossom of the bitter orange tree, although its scent is not at all citrusy. Unfortunately, it is expensive in its pure form, and some people do not like it anyway. Other aromas which have a good relaxing effect are camomile, coriander, geranium, jasmine, lavender, rose and citrus oils. These oils have proved to be useful in combating depression and nervous conditions. They also help in alleviating insomnia and shock.

There are many commercial relaxation tapes available today. Most are a blend of gentle music and a calm voice instructing you to concentrate on picturesque scenes to let your mind drift into a daydream. They work. However, many PTSD sufferers are hypervigilant and have a poor level of concentration. These two symptoms of PTSD make learning to relax with audiotapes a difficult, if not impossible, exercise.

Many PTSD sufferers find themselves with a lot of spare time on their hands. Many are not at work and will be at home, perhaps on their own, for much of the day. In these circumstances it is important to find some form of occupational therapy: to keep busy and to provide some purpose to living. People with nothing to do will soon become fed up and then depressed.

Occupational therapy does not have to be anything elaborate. Taking a general interest in gardening, jogging or cycling might be a start. Those who are less physically active may take up rug-making, tapestry, fishing, reading or writing.

You must do something to occupy your time. If it can be a task with a goal, achieving that goal can be a great boost to your self-esteem. However, the therapy must be something which is realistic, something which is achievable in your present condition. If you are suffering from PTSD your memory may be impaired, your ability to concentrate will be reduced. Physically, your body may protest if you try to do too much, too soon. Being plagued with aching limbs or headaches which force you to abandon your chosen task will do nothing to improve your self-confidence. Choose your occupational therapy wisely.

There are other ways to relax. Perhaps you might like to try a sauna or a Turkish bath. Either of these spa therapies will provide an atmosphere which is conducive to relaxation.

This chapter has not covered every therapy offered to PTSD sufferers because there are too many to explain in one book. For example, EMDR (Eye-movement Desensitisation and Reprocessing Therapy) is a relatively new treatment which has yielded good results with some victims. The introduction of EMDR by Dr Francine Shapiro in 1978, was greeted with excitement mixed with controversy. The process involves talking about the traumatic memory while focusing on the rapidly moving finger of the therapist. The moving finger induces what is described as saccadic eye movements similar to the movements the eye makes when someone is in deep sleep and dreaming. By focusing on the finger and concentrating on the traumatic memory the severity of the trauma is dramatically reduced. There are a number of reliable studies which support EMDR as a treatment (Puffer 1998).

Like all new treatments it is essential that the benefits are validated and accepted by both therapists and their patients. It has been suggested by some researchers (Scott & Palmer, 2000) that EMDR is very similar to the eighteenth century cure of Mesmerism - a psychosocial intervention promoted by the Austrian physician Mesmer.

If a new therapy is offered to you don't dismiss it out of hand. Discuss it with the practitioner who is offering the treatment. Talk to your partner or a close friend. If it feels right then try it. If it works then stick with it. Never simply dismiss a treatment because you "don't like the sound of it". After all, you probably didn't like the sound of PTSD when it was first explained to you!

HOSPITAL

At the time of writing this edition, there are no Health Service beds available for PTSD cases. Not a single bed in UK. However, there are a few private hospitals which do offer in-patient treatment for the most serious cases (Busuttil 2001). Eventually, employers who currently look at injury pensions as a way of removing PTSD victims from employment, may realise that paying for private hospital treatment might be the cheaper alternative in the longer term. It does not take a qualified accountant to realise that a £6,000 course of residential treatment, with an 80% success rate, is a better option than a £10,000 per annum pension for life! But if it is so obvious, why are so few employers prepared to pay for the treatment? The simple answer is that they are unaware of the recovery process from PTSD.

Chapter twelve

Early Interventions
(Debriefing)

Neither Myths nor Miracle Cures

Critical Incident Stress Debriefing (CISD) suffered from a bad press during the period 1994-2001 and a number of people spoke out against the principle that debriefing was a useful tool. I was among those people who were rather sceptical about debriefing. I have now changed my view.

Debriefing is not a cure for PTSD, or an injection against the development of the disorder. Neither does it suggest that all who are involved in a debrief are suffering, or will suffer from the consequences of a trauma. It assumes that after a traumatic incident most people will cope but that they will recover more quickly if they have a structured procedure to follow which helps them to talk about what has happened.

I think my previous scepticism about the principle of debriefing was more to do with the practicalities surrounding the debrief than with the debrief itself.

Do debriefs stick to the rules?
It is generally agreed that debriefing should take place around 36-72 hours after the incident. People's working hours (including shift patterns and days off) and overtime arrangements should be taken into account, but it should run without any breaks (other than brief comfort breaks).

Who does the debrief?
The debriefer may belong to the organisation concerned, or may be independent and contacted through an agency. Increasingly, organisations are training their own personnel as debriefers and this has advantages and disadvantages. The main advantage is

that internally supplied debriefers will know the workings of the organisation very well. The disadvantage is that issues of confidentiality and professionalism may be compromised.

A number of eminent researchers insist that a minimum of two debriefers should be present at any debriefing. However, the debriefing can be for one or more potential victims.

Anecdotal evidence suggests that many trauma victims prefer to be debriefed by someone who is not known to them which usually means a person from outside their organisation. Paradoxically, many organisations prefer to have their own people carry out the debriefing because it is cheaper, and because they feel they have more control over the way the debrief is conducted. The feelings of those needing the debrief are not always taken into consideration. It should be remembered that the cheapest debriefing may not necessarily be the one with the best outcome.

Where is the debrief conducted?

The debrief should take place in a quiet, comfortable venue. Telephones, mobile phones, pagers and all other outside interference should be banned from the room. Refreshments should be available from the very beginning of the time set aside.

Who is invited to the debrief?

This is always a problem. If a debrief becomes too big it is ineffective. However, if people are missing it is also ineffective. It is finding this compromise between the size and effectiveness of the group which forms my greatest misgiving about the exercise. Ideally, everyone closely involved should be present. Therefore, there may be people from within your organisation, and 'outsiders' at the debrief.

People should not be expected to return to work immediately after a debrief.

A problem arises if some people have physical injuries which prevent them attending the debriefing session. They may still be hospitalised so a compromise has to be sought. The debriefing needs to be arranged to allow the maximum number of people to attend. Those who cannot attend because they are too ill, or for other personal reasons, need to be carefully monitored without that monitoring becoming intrusive, counterproductive or offensive.

What time has been set aside for the debriefing?
An average time for a debriefing session is thought to be around three and a half hours. It may be that a session can be quickly wrapped up in a little over one hour. That does not *necessarily* make it a bad debriefing. The largest sections of time during the debriefing should be in establishing the facts of the incident (at least one third of the time) and assessing people's feelings about the incident (at least one third of the time - possibly longer).

What happens after the debriefing?
Refreshments, and a time to approach the debriefer independently. There must be no 'observers' at a debrief. There should be no senior executives to 'monitor' what is said. There should be plenty of time to gather any information about the next stage in the incident - which might be a court case or an inquest. There should be details of where the family and supporters of those involved may seek assistance themselves.

Debriefing can be used for those who experienced one traumatic incident, or for those who have endured more than one incident. Clearly, the more incidents that an individual has experienced then the more complex the debriefing is likely to become, and the greater the risk of suffering from PTSD, or Complex PTSD.

Debriefing must never be viewed as an antidote to PTSD. It is not a magical cure that inoculates victims from the effects of trauma. It is simply a first aid remedy which will, if carried out properly and sympathetically, reduce the risks of victims being diagnosed as suffering from PTSD.

The debriefing should NOT be seen as the end of the matter. *It is not even the beginning of the end. It is simply the end of the beginning.*

Although every debriefing session is slightly different, and those running the sessions will develop the debriefing according to what those present appear to require, there are several generally accepted models for debriefing:- the Mitchell Model, the Dyregrov Model, and a three-stage revised model adapted by such debriefers as Parkinson and others (Parkinson 1997).

My own preference is for an eclectic approach to debriefing as illustrated in the Emotional Decompression Model. The rigidity of sticking to one model is often suffocating the effectiveness of the debriefing.

The four models - in a simple format - are set out here for your interest and for comparison.

Model: The Mitchell Debriefing

1. *Introduction*

2. *Facts*   What happened?

                What did you do?

                How did others treat you?

                How did the incident end?

3. *Thoughts*   What did you think?

                What did you do?

                How did you treat others?

                How did the incident end?

4. *Reactions*   How did you feel in the beginning, and later?

                What was the worst thing about it for you?

                How do you feel now?

5. *Symptoms*   What physical and emotional reactions did you experience:-

                i) at the time?

                ii) later?

6. *Teaching*   Debriefer emphasises the normality of their reactions

                Prepares the debriefees for possible future reactions

7. *Re-entry*   What support is needed?

                What support is available?

                Any questions?

                Issue information and leaflets

                Remain available when debriefing is over

                Follow-up essential; referral as necessary

Time: At least two hours

Model: The Dyregrov Debriefing

1. *Introduction*

2. *Expectations & Facts*

   What happened?

   What did you expect?

   How did others treat you?

   How did the incident end?

3. *Thoughts & sensory impressions*

   What did you think in the beginning and later?

   What did you do, and why?

   What sights, sounds, smells, tastes, touch sensations did you experience?

4. *Emotional reactions*

   How did you feel at the beginning and later?

   What was the worst thing about it for you?

   How do you feel now?

5. *Normalisation*

   Debriefer reassures debriefees of the normality of their reactions

   Explains possible reactions

6. *Future planning & coping*

   What help do you (or your family) need?

   What support do you (or your family) need?

   What have you learned?

7. *Disengagement*

   Any questions?

   Issues, information, leaflets

   Follow-up and referral as necessary

   Debriefer remains behind after session

   Time: minimum of three hours

Model: The Three-stage Revised Debriefing (after Parkinson)

Introduction

Stage 1 *The Facts*   Before   What was happening before the incident?

                       During   What happened during the incident?

                       After   What happened after the incident?

Stage 2 *The Feelings* Sensory impressions

                       Sights, sounds, smells, touch, taste

                       Emotions What feelings and emotions were generated?

                       Reactions What physical reactions?

                       What feelings and reactions are present now?

                       Any positive reactions?

                       Lessons learned?

Stage 3 *The future*   Normalisation

                       Debriefer explains all reactions are normal

                       Gives information about possible reactions

                       Support   Personal, group, organisational, external

                       The aftermath Court cases, inquests, inquiries, funerals

Endings   Final statements

                       Referrals?

                       Refreshments

                       Time: minimum of three hours

Model: Emotional Decompression

Debriefing for Emergency Services/Armed Forces (Kinchin 2004)

Diving in　　Debriefers introduce themselves. Debriefers explain the aim and purpose. Explain the rules and agree them with debriefees.

Stage 1. *Deep water*

Before: What was happening before the incident?

During: What happened during the incident?

After: What happened after the incident?

Stage 2. *Middle water*

Reactions. What physical reactions?

What feelings and reactions are present now?

Any positive reactions?

Lessons learned?

Sensory impressions.

What feelings and emotions were generated?

Stage 3. *Breaking the surface*

Debriefer explains all reactions are normal.

Gives information about possible future reactions.

Coping. Strategies to watch out for.

Snakes & Ladders Model of Recovery explained.

Support: Personal, group, organisational, external.

The aftermath. Court cases, inquests, inquiries, funerals.

Stage 4. *Treading water*

Final statements.

Referrals? Further information. Refreshments.

Time: minimum of 1½ hours

The View Today
During the early stages of the 21st century a "myth", that early intervention was of little or no benefit and may actually harm people, was established. This was in sharp contrast to the needs expressed by traumatised people. Although this "myth" with its resulting debate may help us to critically review the early responses which help people following traumatic events, there is also a grave danger of 'throwing the baby out with the bath water' (Dyregrov 2003).

Early intervention needs to be well organised and structured. It needs to contain more than just provision of comfort and a chance to come together. The services provided for the traumatised must go beyond the provision of debriefing, and should encompass other areas of support appropriate to the needs of the individual client.

We have advanced much more in the field of trauma therapy in recent years than we have done in areas of early intervention. There was a period when too many people, without proper training, were rushing in to do more or less helpful interventions calling these interventions 'debriefing'. These *'ambulance chasers'* gave the whole process a bad name but now the pendulum has swung the other way and people are joining the bandwagon of suggesting that we wait with any form of intervention. This debate does have one major consequence. It has led to a more flexible view of early intervention and driven away some of the hard and fast rules which were previously, and erroneously, applied to all situations.

The Biology of PTSD - Dual Attention Theory
One of the newer theories about trauma is Brewins (2001) dual attention theory which has been supplemented by Turnbull (2003). It is postulated that there are two different memory systems, one called the verbally accessible memory (VAM) and the other situational or sensory accessible memory (SAM). While the first system uses the verbal mode and contains easily accessible memory information that can be communicated to others through language and speech the SAM system contains personal perception-based information dependent upon the different sensory channels. Information is not verbally encoded

and is harder to communicate to others. The 'bridge' joining the two memories is the hippocampus which acts like a fuse. This fuse may be damaged or destroyed during a traumatic event and so prevent the VAM and SAM memory systems sharing information.

Flashbacks are one way of gradually allowing SAM memories into the VAM system and then integrating them into the memories of past and present. As the hippocampus recovers so the number and intensity of flashbacks will decrease.

It is suggested that whilst these hippocampus 'bridges' are destroyed and flashbacks are at their height, debriefing is ineffective and may even be harmful as a re-exposure to the trauma. Waiting for the regeneration of the hippocampus may take as long as one month. Therefore it may be logical and sensible to delay debriefing by as much as one month in some cases.

The Eclectic Approach to Early Intervention

Now that the dust is settling following the debate which developed the "myth" of bad early intervention, it is time to move forward and provide best practice for those in need of support. Best practice should include good quality early intervention.

The term 'debriefing' has been damaged by this debate and it has been suggested that it should even be replaced (Raphael 2000). The umbrella term 'early intervention' is now more readily used but other phrases are starting to appear in texts. My own feeling is that the term "Emotional Decompression" is appropriate and to many the word decompression suggests a staged approach to a recovery situation.

There is also a need for a flexible approach that has a structure which allows for adaptation to individual needs rather than being prescriptive and rigid (Tehrani 2002). Much of the "myth" about debriefing came about because it was researched in isolation. Indeed in some cases it was used as a therapy in isolation. Early interventions should not be used in isolation but must form a part of a carefully managed care package for those who are traumatised. Within the framework of the post-trauma care package there is a most definite need for early interventions along the lines of those commonly called debriefing.

My own view has changed since the publication of the previous edition of this book. From being very sceptical of debriefing as a process I have become very supportive of early interventions.

The approach to - debriefing - early intervention - emotional decompression - should be an eclectic one. In the same way that trauma counsellors have access to a number of different and complementary counselling theories, those who practice early interventions should work in much the same way.

The strict ruling about the timing of any intervention should be disregarded. There is plenty of anecdotal evidence to suggest that a carefully tailored debriefing can be offered to a client two days, two weeks, two months or even two years after the initial trauma. Indeed, it is logical if the Dual Attention Theory is applied then a significant number of debriefings may take place around one month after the trauma.

During training sessions for debriefers, which I have facilitated, it has become clear that far too many experienced debriefers have become frustrated by the rules which they were originally happy to comply with. At the end of the course, delegates have been refreshed by the knowledge that they can (if they want to) sit clients around a table to debrief them. They can delay a debriefing by three or four days in order to get the full shift of officers together in one place at one time.   They can use the Mitchell Model for one debriefing and then shift to another model, if they feel it is more appropriate, for another debriefing. Indeed, they can take the elements from all the available debriefing models and compose their own model with which they are confident and comfortable. The object is to offer best practice to the clients, not pay homage to a particular model of treatment.

Looking at the time taken to complete a debriefing session, this may vary from a little over an hour to as much as four hours duration. Debriefing a small group of well trained emergency service staff may only take 60 minutes. Debriefing *one* rape victim may take all day.

Training for debriefers

The training of debriefers has suffered because there is no standard, and currently there is no such thing as an *accredited debriefer*. Looking at the work of the British Psychological Society and their report on Psychological Debriefing (Tehrani 2002) it is clear that there are vast differences in the training of debriefers both nationally and internationally.

Setting a standard for debriefing training and for the clinical supervision of debriefers may be some way off. I am concerned that those who attempt to set the standards have their own agendas for doing so (perhaps I have my own agenda too) but something along the lines suggested here may be appropriate:-

	Initial Training	Five day course
Year 1	Annual update	One day refresher
Year 2	Biannual refresher	Three day course
Year 3	Annual update	One day refresher
Year 4	Biannual refresher	Three day course

Supervision of individual debriefers - after every three debriefing sessions or annually if fewer sessions have been facilitated during that time. The supervision could form part of the annual one day update. Currently it would appear that very few debriefers receive the level of clinical supervision they should expect and require.

Code of Ethics for Debriefing

At the time of writing, no such code exists. That is a gap which needs to be filled. Currently, the work of debriefers relies upon the integrity of those individuals and those organisations which provide the service.

The "Myth"

The "myth" that debriefing is bunkum has been blown away for good. However, the situation may return if better training and support for debriefers is not sought and the quest for 'best practice' is not maintained.

Early interventions, such as debriefing, are neither myths nor miracle cures. They can greatly assist those who have suffered from exposure to a trauma so long as they are correctly applied and they form part of a complete trauma care package.

Chapter thirteen

Recovery from PTSD

Perhaps the most common question asked by PTSD survivors is "When will I get better?" It is a perfectly natural question. If a person suffers an appendicitis or a broken leg there is a typical recovery period and there are definite stages before good health is regained. Stitches are removed or the plaster cast is taken off. With PTSD there are no such readily identifiable stages of recovery, and each individual's progress will be different.

In many ways, PTSD sufferers find themselves playing a game of emotional snakes and ladders. The game board represents the road to recovery, divided into one hundred squares. A series of ladders helps the person on the way towards recovery but between these ladders are the snakes which may take the victim backwards towards the start of the game, experiencing previous anguish and turmoil.

The Snakes and Ladders Model of Recovery

The traumatic event takes place on square one. From this position recovery begins. Some survivors may shake the dice scoring five, four, three, and then one to reach square 100, thus achieving recovery in just four shakes of the dice. In less than four weeks these persons have recovered from an acute stress reaction (ASR) and they do NOT go on to develop PTSD. Other survivors have to journey around the board going up the ladders and down the snakes as they slowly progress to the end of the game. Tragically, a few people may never finish the game.

Furthermore, they may never roll the correct number on the dice to finish exactly on square 100, or more tragically, they may give up and walk away from the game board taking unrelinquished trauma with them.

The game of snakes and ladders is very complex. Study the game board in detail. It is possible for a player to be on square 97, only to shake a one, two, five, five, five and one. These throws take a player back to square 4! Thankfully, on a true snakes and ladders board no snake can take a person all the way back to square one.

Diagram: Snakes & Ladders Model of Recovery (Kinchin 1994, 1998)

So a person can finish the game in four moves, or can be taken back 94 squares in just six moves. Describing PTSD in such a way may aid a greater insight into the complicated road to recovery from PTSD. This analogy is probably more realistic than the very simple idea that recovery is a case of two steps forward and then one step back. Recovery is not smooth. Neither is it predictable and it will incorporate a wealth of stages which extend far beyond the models described by such researchers as Williams (1993) and Horowitz (1979).

Examples of Snakes and Ladders which might affect a person's recovery are described below:

Ladders
- Good medication, such as antidepressants, can be seen as an essential aid to recovery for many child survivors. The withdrawal of medication has to be slow and sympathetic or this 'ladder' can quickly become a 'snake'.
- Therapy which includes counselling, and any other form of support in which the survivor has confidence (Kinchin 1997).
- Relaxation techniques can be taught, and practised.
- Realisation that there is a "trauma bond" or a the feeling of empathy which exists between those who have suffered traumatic events. It is a realisation that "you are not alone", and "you are not going mad".
- Individual or group support is an essential part of recovery.

Snakes
- Panic attacks can become a major 'snake' in the path of recovery. Because the fear of panic is so great many survivors develop avoidance strategies in an attempt to stay

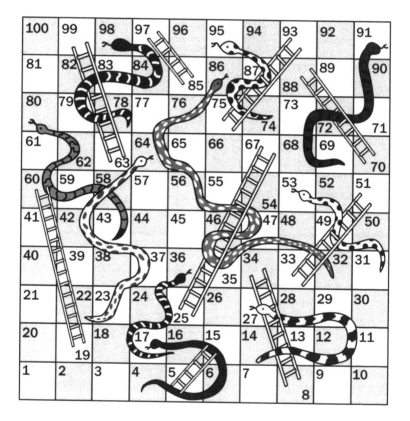

away from anything which might cause a panic attack.

- Depression can manifest itself any time. A deep trough of depression can cause a survivor to walk away from the game board altogether. Consequently, this is the most dangerous 'snake' of all.

- Alcohol & non-prescribed drugs can act as an initial 'crutch', but dependency on these products can seriously hinder any real progress towards recovery. This is particularly true of adolescent survivors.

- Adverse publicity can heighten the state of a survivor's feelings of guilt.
- Anniversaries are often obstacles, but a successfully handled anniversary can also be turned into a positive milestone towards recovery.
- Non-acceptance of PTSD by professionals and lay persons can be a serious problem for survivors who feel the severity of the traumatic response is being disregarded or belittled.

The examples above illustrate some of the events and issues which may affect anyone on the road to recovery. Many PTSD sufferers and their carers tend to set themselves goals or targets. Often these targets will be linked to the calendar:

- 'I will return to school by 1st June'
- 'I want to have stopped sleeping with the main light on by Christmas'
- 'I intend to go out shopping on my own during my holiday'

Formulating goals and targets is a good strategy provided the targets are within reach. If the target is too difficult, then the sufferer is in danger of setting unrealistic goals which serve no useful purpose. Rather, sufferers should be encouraged to set themselves sensible, attainable, targets. Dates for accomplishing tasks should be within a reasonable time scale. If the target is reached before the date, a treat may act as a positive reward. For children in particular, it is vital they are enabled to achieve small steps towards recovery.

Inevitably, some targets will not be achieved. Life is full of unpredictable events which may hinder progress. That's life! Therefore, unexpected events should be allowed for in the preparation of targets and breathing spaces need to be allowed between achieving a goal and embarking on the next hurdle. Targets are wonderful when they are achieved, but terrible if the survivor is defeated by them.

The snakes and ladders board can act as a helpful reminder to the survivor of their journey towards recovery. If he fails to reach a target, that failure does not drag him all the way back to square one. Even in failing, he has learned something about how best to set the next target.

Full recovery

It is not necessary to reach square 100 on the snakes and ladders board to have recovered from PTSD. Indeed, I suggest that in some cases reaching square 100 is not possible. Witnessing or being involved in a seriously traumatic event affects the rest of a survivor's life. This may require a person rethinking life-goals or life-values. Perhaps it would be useful to consider full recovery as anything beyond square 91 on the game board. Thus, in the example of a broken leg cited earlier, there is always the thought in the back of a person's mind that the leg could break again. Likewise with PTSD, some of the symptoms could be awakened if triggers occur. Therefore, reaching the top nine squares on the snakes and ladders board, whilst being aware of the remaining two snakes, may be perceived as recovery.

Errors of information processing in PTSD cases (after Scott & Palmer [2000] and others)

Although there are now a significant number of books and papers on the subject of Post Traumatic Stress Disorder, and suggestions for diagnostic and treatment techniques, very few give any practical comments about recovery. Where PTSD is discussed, evidence is generally anecdotal and has been gleaned from the hundreds of PTSD survivors who have volunteered information as a way of supporting others and affirming their own identifiable milestones in recovery.

Occasionally, PTSD victims have encountered the following difficulties:-

- Making unreasonable generalisations, eg All men are sexual abusers. Every teacher is a bully.
- Mentally filtering aspects of their trauma, eg Seizing on a particularly gloomy aspect of an event and dwelling on it. "He could have been killed doing that."
- Believing 'all or nothing', eg Everything is seen in the most extreme terms - "I am either in control or I am not."
- Labelling and mis-labelling themselves, eg Individuals

focusing on their emotional state and drawing conclusions about themselves, "Since it happened, I am frightened of my own shadow, I guess I'm just a wimp."

- A discounting attitude, eg Disregarding any positive outcomes, for example "I did my best, so what?"
- Magnification and minimisation of self-worth, eg Magnification of shortcomings and making light of strengths. "Since the trauma I'm so irritable with my children, and just about manage to get them to school."
- Making 'should' statements. Inappropriate use of moral imperatives - should - must - have - ought, eg "It's ridiculous that since the attack I now have to take my sister shopping with me. I should be able to do this by myself."
- Jumping to conclusions, eg "Everyone thinks I should be over this by now."
- Over-personalisation of the situation. Assuming that because something went wrong it must be the survivor's fault, eg "I must have made a mistake somewhere for him to have died."

Revised thinking by PTSD survivors in advanced recovery (Quinton, Kinchin and others)

Recovery is very difficult to assess. There are tests which provide a 'score' indicating the depth of traumatic experience. Therefore, if a test is administered and the survivor achieves a 'low score' it may be assumed a survivor is no longer traumatised and has recovered.

However, recovery is more a state of mind than it is a score in any psychoanalytical test. Recovery is a sense of achievement when something previously considered impossible becomes achievable and the victim feels it is well within grasp.

Recovery might include a person being able to think:

- I'm not so hard on myself these days.
- Things can be divided into what really matters, and what doesn't really matter.
- I catch myself refocusing on the present.
- I can share with others.
- I have learned to cherish laughter.

- The pain of what happened has immunised me against most petty hurts.
- I focus on the present and the near future. I leave the past in the past.
- I am stronger because of what happened to me.
- I can use what happened to me to support others.
- Life has new meaning for me.
- I am starting to get bored with my story about the attack.
- My memories do not go away, but they are losing their gripping quality.
- My memories are no longer able to stop me in my tracks. I have control over them.
- I have the choice now; I can choose to leave it (the traumatic memory) if I want to.
- I can bear the pain of what happened.

Recovery from PTSD is akin to recovery from grief (Worden 1991). It is possible and indeed normal for a person to reach a health resolution to their grief. But the memory of the deceased person is still very real. Likewise, the memory of the trauma will remain for the PTSD victim. There will still be some remaining scar tissue. A child survivor of trauma may well have suffered academically and will have some catching-up to do if he wishes to regain his previous status with his peer group. This catching-up with academic work may be a realistic hurdle rather than an attempt to control the traumatic memory. Conversely, the fact that a child is still two reading books behind his classmates, or is some way behind with her mathematics project work, may serve as a reminder of the trauma and the consequences of being traumatised. Consequently, periods of depression, or even relapses into a state of traumatisation may result.

In the same way that a bereaved person may re-experience feelings of grief at anniversaries or other special moments, so a traumatised person may endure a brief re-experiencing of some traumatic symptoms.

Recovery from Complex PTSD (PDSD)
For those survivors who are recovering from Complex PTSD then the snakes and ladders model can still be applied. However, these victims of abuse or repeated traumas should

imagine that they have several counters on the game-board instead of the usual one. The counters have to be moved independently, each with its own shake of the dice. In this way, one or two counters may reach the top of the board a considerable way ahead of the others. This is how recovery from Complex PTSD is. However, it can been seen that recovery is just as possible, but may take a little longer to achieve.

I believe that the Snakes and Ladders Model is an approach which can be applied to all individuals because:

- It allows for the oscillations in recovery.
- It is easy to comprehend since almost everyone has some knowledge of the snakes and ladders game.
- The process of recovery is easily explained.
- Although the snakes and ladders model appears to be very simple the model also demonstrates the complexity of PTSD, and allows for extremes of the disorder (C-PTSD) to be worked into the same model.

Chapter fourteen

Personal stories

What happened to the eleven cases?

Chapter 2 introduced eleven victims of trauma and described in their own words the particular trauma they faced (Caruth 1995). Following on from that, many of the people have added comments at various points in the text to illustrate a variety of issues and problem areas.

Since their exposure to trauma, what has become of these people? How has their experience affected their life? Do they continue to suffer from Post Traumatic Stress Disorder?

CASE 1: DAVID

I was attacked by a group of youths whilst on duty as a police officer. The attack left me with a broken cheekbone, a damaged kidney and spleen, and PTSD. The attack occurred in July 1990.

I spent five days in hospital after the attack. I thought I would start to feel better when I got home, but my own doctor started talking about Post Traumatic Stress Disorder. He explained that my 'restlessness' was all due to the attack and that I was constantly reliving the incident in my mind.

I then started the counselling. At first it was at home as I was in no fit state to travel. Then as the days went by I was asked to visit the hospital for my counselling therapy.

I was not sleeping, I was so jumpy it was ridiculous. I could not concentrate on anything for more than a few minutes, and my memory was terrible. I started to get flashbacks of the attack. They were vivid pictures of the incident. I found them extremely distressing.

After two months it became obvious to me that I was not much better. I was then offered a stay at the police convalescent home. While there I met other PTSD sufferers and I started to gain a different perspective of the condition. I was introduced to aromatherapy, physiotherapy and hypnotism. I swam, exercised in a gym and relaxed in a sauna.

I returned home from convalescence realising that it was possible to recover from PTSD but that it was going to take time. I had also accepted the fact that I was going to have to take some medication to help me combat the symptoms of the condition.

Nine months after the attack I returned to police duties. It was hard. So much had changed, even the station photocopier was in a different location. I was given a job in the training department, so had no direct contact with the public. I set to work at my new task.

I had been at work for just three months when my father-in-law died. This added extra strain to family life and affected me far more that I had expected. I had to take time off work. The week after his death was the first anniversary of my assault.

I went back to work briefly but found I had no interest in what I was doing. I started to find excuses for finishing early. I had not told anyone, but in all my time at work I had avoided using a police radio. I also stopped using the telephone. This was making life very difficult.

By October 1991 I'd had enough of pretending. I had changed so much there was no way I could continue to work for the police. I was placed on sick leave pending retirement and was medically retired in April 1992.

Freed from the expectations of returning to police duties I started to make a better recovery. My sleeping improved but I was still troubled by my inability to use the telephone or to mix in crowded situations.

I started to write for magazines and newspapers. Nothing too spectacular, but one published feature tended to spark off another idea. By the end of the first 12 months I had been published in over 20 different publications both in Britain and the United States. I had also had a radio play produced in South Africa.

Much of my writing was linked to PTSD and my own experiences. As much as anything else it was therapeutic. I started to research the subject in university and hospital libraries, and I soon discovered that there was not much literature available to PTSD sufferers.

In April 1993, I agreed with a publisher to produce a practical guide for PTSD sufferers. The project was to take up the next 15 months of my life, and help me to come to terms with the fact that the trauma of 1990 had permanently affected my life. But it had unknowingly provided me with the opportunity to do something I had wanted to do for many years - write.

1997 update: Things have progressed well for me. In 1994 I decided that I needed to return to a working environment, just to prove that I could. I obtained a job-share in the library of an Oxford college and combined this work with my writing.

Within two years the writing work was growing so rapidly that I decided to reduce the hours I worked in the library. Writing, and presenting seminars about PTSD became my primary occupations.

Perhaps one of the most exciting events I attended was the inaugural meeting of a PTSD support group called ASSIST. I was told that the founders of this group felt inspired to help PTSD sufferers after reading my book and I was to be their guest speaker! This boosted my own self-esteem as well as helping others who were suffering from the same disorder that had changed my life. This meeting was a vivid example of the "trauma bond" actively at work.

I still suffer from the odd moody day. I am still aware that my life has been changed by just one traumatic event. However, the difference is that I can now live happily with that knowledge and have full control of the terrible memory. At least, that is how it now feels.

ASSIST can be contacted by letter: 11 Albert Street, Rugby, Warwickshire CV21 2RX, UK, or by telephone: 01788 560800.

CASE 2: MARLENE

Marlene had worked in the armed services and a hospital as a nurse and was no stranger to seeing casualties. Then she was involved in two motoring accidents. In both cases she was the innocent party and had no control over what happened. The accidents happened in December 1990 and January 1993.

After the first accident I spent two days in hospital and was then discharged. I was back at work within a month and thought very little about it.

The second accident was different somehow. It made me realise how lucky I was to be alive. My life had come so close to ending. I spent six days in hospital. For most of that time I was a wreck. I kept bursting into tears at the slightest thing. I could picture both accidents clearly in my mind. Then the two started to blur together into one long incident. It was as if everyone on the road was out to get me.

When I was released from hospital I hated the journey home in my friend's car. I sat in my kitchen and remember thinking that I never wanted to go outside again. I couldn't bear the thought of walking along the street to the local store. I certainly did not want to drive there.

I relied a lot on friends helping me out. They got my groceries in for me and did all sorts of other chores. Then their patience started to wear thin. One or two stopped visiting.

One day I was standing at the window watching the rain. I remembered how heavy the rain had been that caused the first accident. Then I realised that it had been months since I had been out in the rain - I had been avoiding it. My supervisor from work called to see me and she arranged for me to see a counsellor. The counsellor came to my home. I talked about the rain, about being a passenger in a car. I explained how frightened I was about going outside. Then I told her about the flashbacks I was having: the wakeful nights, the bad temper - the list of moans appeared to have no end.

By the time I had finished she was smiling at me. She said that what I was experiencing was all perfectly normal. I had survived two very traumatic events. On both occasions I was nearly killed. Naturally I was worried that the third time anything happened I would die. So to make sure I was safe, I stayed at home.

It all sounded so silly when she described it like that, but she was absolutely right.

Over the next few weeks I saw a lot of my counsellor. She encouraged me to go out in a cab for a ride around the block. I panicked for most of the journey but when I got back home I felt so pleased with myself. The cab rides got longer and then I tried one on my own. Even the drivers were good to me. Nobody laughed. I remembered thinking that me and cars must be the same as Vietnam veterans and helicopters.

I kept a scrapbook of my thoughts and my steps to recovery. I also learned how to relax. I went to aromatherapy classes and found the sessions a great help. I immediately bought my own supply of oils and started to read up on the subject. Before I knew it, I was becoming an expert on aromatherapy.

The flashbacks diminished and my sleeping improved. I decided to give up nursing and went back to college to train as an aromatherapist. I could see my life in a new light.

By the end of 1994 I shall be set up in my own practice, teaching people the benefits of natural oils. I still remember the accidents as I drive my car along busy roads. The incidents have changed my life, but I'm enjoying every minute of it now.

1997 update: Business is good. I enjoy working for myself in my own practice and setting my own agenda. The accidents feel a long time ago now, almost as if they had happened to someone else - another me.

I've moved from Washington State across the border into Canada and have a lovely house on the outskirts of Vancouver. There is even a bit of romance in the air, but I'm not going to tell you about that.

CASE 3: GRAHAM

Whilst travelling to an emergency incident in his Fire Chief's car, Graham found his role suddenly changed. One moment he was the rescuer, the next he was a victim. The brick which was thrown at his speeding car changed his life significantly.

After the 'accident' my memory became very vague. Now, I'm not sure how much I can remember and how much I've been told by other people. It is all one big jumble in my mind.

Because of my head and shoulder injuries, I was kept in hospital for eight days. The incident made all the local papers and the TV news. I kept all the press cuttings but I hardly ever look at them. I will one day.

My recovery went well for three or four months. I returned to work, doing an office job as a senior Fire Prevention Officer. Then one day, I was asked to go to the scene of an incident and give advice to the crew who were dealing with it.

Speeding through the town with the blue lights flashing started to jolt my memory. I was on different roads, but every time I came to a bridge I slowed down and studied the area for would-be brick throwers. I got slower and slower. In the end I turned off the blue lights and pulled to the side of the road. I sat there and cried my eyes out.

It was as if the clock had been turned back four months. Everything was so clearly imprinted in my mind. I could see the brick coming towards my car - over and over again.

Eventually I realised they were calling me on the radio. I acknowledged the call and said I was having mechanical trouble. I found my way to the incident and got some questioning looks from one or two officers there. As soon as I could I went back to my office, hung up my uniform and went home.

I had two terrible nights when I just couldn't sleep. In the end I went to the doctor and said I had sleep problems and a lot of headaches. He talked to me for some time, asking all kinds of questions. I got very irritable with him; shouting and pacing up and down his office. Then I slumped down in the chair and cried again.

He told me what was wrong: Post Traumatic Stress Disorder. I thought that only affected people who were involved in large-scale incidents. He put me straight on a few things and explained how the drive under all those bridges in my Fire Chief's car had triggered off all the hidden memories of the trauma I had experienced: the incident in which I nearly died. He said I needed some time off work and gave me a certificate for three months sick leave!

Looking back at it all now, it was that long period of sick leave which made me realise that PTSD was not a two-minute illness. I was going to have to work at recovering from this condition.

I started going swimming. I went cycling. I went on long and lonely walks. I found myself doing all kinds of things so that I could be on my own. I distanced myself from the family and felt numb. I rarely laughed or cried. I just drifted in a world of my own.

After two months of this I agreed to see a counsellor. She counselled me with many other firemen who had been diagnosed as suffering from PTSD. After lots of background questions she started to quiz me about the incident. I always tried to avoid the subject, but she carefully steered me back to it each time we met.

At about the same time I agreed to take some pills the doctor offered me. He explained that my body needed a break. I was stressed, very tired, very anxious and slightly depressed. I would need medical help to overcome this.

I was given a further three months off work.

My counsellor introduced me to three other people who were suffering from Post Traumatic Stress Disorder. We met as a group on several occasions. It was such a relief to find that I was not alone with my problems - other people who experienced totally different incidents appeared to suffer from the same symptoms.

I started to keep a diary. It was just a note of how I felt each day, what I did and what I postponed doing. I started to make myself do things so that I got out and met people. However, I got really sick of neighbours asking, 'How are you?' I'm sure they didn't really want to know. The trouble was, I had no visible means of being identified as ill. My injuries were invisible.

The Fire Service were very understanding about everything. There was no pressure to return to work before I was ready. The only pressure was from me. I felt guilty about not being at work.

My 50th birthday approached and I discussed with my wife the idea of taking early retirement. We had saved a considerable sum of money and had always wanted to move to Australia to live near our son and his family. We played around with the idea for several months before making the decision. It appeared that the incident had made both of us see life in a different way. We wanted to be positive about the future.

In the meantime, I had returned to part-time work in Fire Prevention. To be honest, I didn't do very much, but it kept me occupied. The counselling continued, but only once a month by this time. I kept in contact with the others in my counselling group. They were all making slow, but steady progress.

I retired in March 1993, four and a half years after the incident. We moved out to Australia and I now have a part-time consultancy job with a company selling fire equipment. I feel closer than ever to my wife, and we are living only sixty miles from the rest of our family.

When I look back on the incident now there is no sorrow. It gave me the chance to think about the rest of my life and what I wanted to do. Occasionally, I have a sleepless night, and sometimes I panic slightly at the sight of a bridge. But I don't let these things bother me any more. I am too busy opening the shutters to each new day.

1997 update: Things were going very well but then I was taken ill. In August 1997 I was admitted into hospital because I suffered a "fit". Everyone was very worried. In fact it was a panic attack. Doctors came and went and eventually one of them told me it was Post Traumatic Stress Disorder. This was terrible. I thought I was over it all. The flashbacks were there again.

I spent three days in hospital coming to terms with the fact that I was still suffering from PTSD. I had stopped driving again. I couldn't face sitting in the driving seat. I found it hard to believe that after nine years this thing could still come back and haunt me in this way. Then my wife reminded me of the snakes and ladders board. We looked in the Guinness Book or Records and decided that I had just slipped down the longest snake in the world - a python! I hope that being able to laugh at that is the first step towards the nearest ladder.

CASE 4: CINDY

For several months after the accident Cindy refused to admit to herself that anything was different. Having a ladder fall on you was no big deal, she would say. However, her friends knew differently. They saw the changes taking place in her character. The lecturers at college also noticed a difference.

I just wanted to pick up life where I had left off. I didn't miss much at college and soon caught up with the rest of the class. People kept inviting me out to parties, to music concerts and the like. I usually felt too tired and told them I suffered from headaches because of the accident. I stopped colouring my hair and let it all grow. It was too much effort to keep the Mohican style looking good.

Eventually my mum commented on the fact that I never went out any more. I thought about that. Mum was right. I was almost frightened to go out of the house. I even dreaded going to college. I was becoming agoraphobic.

I started to read up on phobias. It didn't really make sense. Mine was not an irrational fear, it was all due to that blasted ladder falling on me. Before that I was fine.

I started to get depressed. I also started to drink. I think dad noticed the drink disappearing, but he didn't say anything to me.

Then one morning they came home and found me drunk. Drunk at 11 am! Mum put me to bed and made all sorts of 'tut-tut' noises. The next day I made straight for the drinks cupboard, only to find it locked! I hunted high and low for the key but couldn't find it. I didn't even know what it looked like. Why had they locked it?

I knew the answer really, but couldn't bring myself to admit it. I sat and cried, then started to take stock of my life. My marks at college were steadily going down. One or two comments were made about that. I never went out. I drank too much and I was always moody.

Six months after the accident I had to return to hospital for a check-up. I sat in the out-patients department for ages waiting to be seen. It was very busy and I kept moving from seat to seat to so as to stay away from other patients. I always sat with my back to a wall and never stopped watching the rest of the room. I started to think about the accident. I had changed since it had happened. So what!

The doctor finally saw me. He looked shocked at the sight of me. Funny really because I looked more 'normal' at that time that at any stage in the last three years.

He started off by asking how long I had been drinking heavily. He said I was shaking badly and I stank of stale booze. Talk about being subtle. He just came out with it all.

After a few moments I started to unwind and tell him about the drink, about quiet nights at home and the poor marks at college. I then waited for him to give me the 'pull yourself together' lecture, but it didn't come.

He started to ask all sorts of questions about my day-to-day life. I answered them without really thinking about what he was leading up to. He then asked me to wait as he wanted me to see another doctor.

The other doctor turned out to be a psychiatrist. I was livid. They thought I was nuts!

Eventually I calmed down. The psychiatrist started talking to me about the accident. I went through the whole story again. Then he asked why I never went out with my friends, and why I drank. I had to struggle to answer those. I didn't know myself.

At the end of all this he talked me into coming back in two days' time to see a colleague of his. She would spend some time talking things through with me. In the meantime he wanted me to try to cut right down on the drinking.

It was not until the third meeting with the counsellor that the subject of Post Traumatic Stress was mentioned. I had never heard of it, and so she explained that my agoraphobia, heavy drinking, depression and poor concentration at college were all linked to the accident. The tough bit was that I would have to stop drinking so that they could help me with all the other symptoms.

The counselling sessions progressed and the drinking eased and then stopped. It was hard going, though. Eventually I told my parents what was happening. They were so relieved. It transpired that they knew I was not well but that every time they said anything I just bit their heads off. They were worried that I would leave home, or 'do something silly' because I was clearly feeling fed-up. Being honest with my parents made everything else so much easier to deal with.

The counselling worked out and the phobic behaviour improved. I stopped drinking. My dad took me out to a pub for a drink. We went into the crowded bar and I ordered a fruit juice. When we came out I was so excited with the achievement that I'm sure everyone else thought I was drunk. My dad just grinned from ear to ear.

Things progressed steadily. I finished college with the required piece of paper and got a job not too far from home. I now have a boyfriend, and things in that department are pretty serious. We are planning a honeymoon in Florida.

1997 update: Unfortunately, I have been unable to contact Cindy to update this story. There is nothing sinister in that fact. I know that the wedding and the honeymoon in Florida took place but I have lost contact since then. Cindy probably has better things to do!

CASE 5: MATTHEW

The suicide of his closest friend, followed by a burglary in his own home affected Matthew. It is not easy to establish which event induced the PTSD, and so it was assumed that both occurrences were equally to blame.

I found John's suicide very difficult to cope with. For weeks I held myself responsible. I should have noticed how depressed he had become. I didn't. I saw John and myself as very much alike. We were almost like brothers. We did everything together. I missed him terribly.

The burglary was the trigger that sent my mind racing back to John's death. Slowly I realised that what had really frightened me was the thought that John had been murdered and that the killer might still be in the house waiting for me. When I was burgled, this all came back to me and I thought that the murderer had returned for me.

It all sounds so silly now. But months of careful counselling brought all this out into the open. When I was a kid, someone in our street was shot dead. I saw the body in the street before the police arrived. Clearly, the closeness of these deaths had an effect upon me. The more I think about it the more convinced I become that the brain has got a separate mind of its own. It stores things for years.

I started to become very depressed - really low. I never tried to kill myself, but I think I came close to it on a few occasions.

The depression eased with medication. However, it was replaced by the side-effects of the drugs. My doctor tried me on five different types of antidepressant before he found one that I could live with.

I have been taking these tablets for two years now. Soon I will have to start reducing the doses and seeing how I feel. I tried once before and the depression returned.

I also suffered a lot from panic attacks. I found public transport the worst. You can never be in control of the situation on public transport. When I visited Europe I was really pleased with myself for coping on the airliner. Then the incident on the London Underground blew all that confidence away.

I am slowly learning to control the panics. Sometimes I do so by simply avoiding the situation, but more and more I am prepared to try things to see if I can cope. I remember the analogy of the snakes and ladders board, and that helps me overcome the failures. There is always the next time.

Since the burglary I have changed job three times. I don't find it easy to settle into new situations but I am sure that, too, will improve given time.

Even all this time after John's death, different things spark off the memory of the day I broke into his home. Each time a dog barks I think of John's dog. When the telephone rings I often think of my search for John's telephone. When I hear glass breaking (usually a TV sound effect) I recall how I broke into John's home. All these triggers make it difficult for me to relax during the day. I am always alert and waiting for the next event to spark off a memory.

Looking back through my diaries I can see that I have improved considerably over the last two years. Although events still spark off sad memories, they do not set off the awful panic attacks I used to have. Probably those around me are totally unaware that I am panicking about something. I relax myself by concentrating on my breathing and letting my arms hang loose.

I am sure that, given a little more time, continued guidance from my counsellor, and the maintained support of my doctor, that I will crack the PTSD. The memory of John's death will always be with me. But when I think of him I also remember all the good times.

1997 update: I was right. The memory of John is a happy one. I don't think about him every day any more. But I haven't forgotten him. My life has returned to normal and the incident is almost forgotten - unless I want to think about it, like now. That is the difference. I am now in control of the memory. It does not jump out of my mind and hit me with fear like it used to. All in all, things are looking good.

CASE 6: JESSICA

Following her Caesarean section, Jessica and her baby daughter returned home. Jessica was in a terrible state. She suffered symptoms of agoraphobia and a fear of the telephone. But in 1981 few people understood PTSD. Jessica was very much on her own.

I started having nightmares. These doctors with knives in their hands were walking towards me. I was terrified.

Every time the telephone rang I had a panic attack. I couldn't go outside for a walk because I thought these doctors would be waiting for me. I had my hands full looking after my baby.

I kept going back to my doctor. My husband made me go the first few times. The doctor said that I was depressed and that this was a normal reaction. He thought that I was disappointed at missing out on a natural birth.

I took tablets on and off for years. I went back to my part-time job when my daughter started school. It was a real struggle but I forced myself to do it.

Then one day my own doctor was on holiday and I saw somebody else. He suggested that I saw a psychologist which I agreed to do without giving it much thought. After a couple of discussions with the psychologist he suggested that I might be suffering from Post Traumatic Stress Disorder. This was in 1988, seven years after my daughter was born.

The psychologist took me back in time and talked about my pregnancy and the birth of my daughter. I described the wait outside the theatre suite and how frightened I was. He said that most people were frightened of operations and that my extra wait outside the theatre had magnified my fears. He said that my reaction was normal.

My daughter is now studying for exams, and my husband and I are really contented with life. Now I know what my problems are, I am overcoming them steadily. Admittedly, I still take mild antidepressants from time to time. But I don't worry about taking them. I know they make me feel much better. I get out and about like everyone else and I use the telephone if I have to.

1997 update: My daughter is still at school and doing well. I am much happier and even do some work with mothers who have difficulty getting to know and love their new babies. I have met other mothers who had traumatic times giving birth and even came across an organisation that believes in PTBSD, Post Traumatic Birth Stress Disorder.

Knowing that others have found birth a traumatic experience has made me realise that I am normal. It was the circumstances of the birth that were abnormal.

It is possible to contact other PTSD or PTBSD sufferers by contacting the Trauma After Care Trust (TACT). It is so good to talk to other people who understand your problem.

TACT, Buttfields, The Farthings, Withington, Gloucestershire GL54 4DF, UK, Tel 01242 890306.

CASE 7: RICHARD
Following a fire which threatened to destroy an entire family, Richard found that reminders of the event prevented him from doing his job as a police officer effectively. This was a problem he had to overcome.

I returned to work two days after the fire. It was all I could think about. Pictures of it kept filling my mind. It was impossible to last a day at work without something reminding me of the way those people were nearly burned alive before my eyes.

August is usually a social amble from one barbecue to another. But this year I just couldn't stand the sight and smells and had to walk out of friends' homes on several occasions. My wife got pretty sick of this and told me so in no uncertain terms. I explained the reasons behind it and she stared at me in horror. I then told her about the fire in detail. She only knew what she had read in the papers and most of that was rubbish.

The police training exercise where I had a row with the instructor was the last straw. I knew I needed help to overcome this thing, but there was no way I was going to tell anyone in the police what was troubling me.

I saw a trauma counsellor and she started to put everything into perspective for me. It had taken five months for me to make the appointment, however, and in that time I had started to avoid situations that I knew would remind me of the fire. Now I find that these avoidances had become habits that were difficult to break.

Initially, having the counselling brought all the flashbacks back as vividly as ever. The counsellor said this might happen and that, although painful, it was a good indication that I had started to deal with the trauma. However, I found that the return of these vivid images depressed me and made me anxious that I might never get any better.

Going over the details of the fire with my counsellor was painful, but it started to work for me in the end. I could picture the family trapped behind the bars at the window without panicking - after all, I knew that they got out safely so why did I need to panic?

I felt that I had a terrible lack of confidence. I lost the ability to accept normal negative events, and looked for occasions where I had failed. I started to see my failings all around. Nothing I appeared to do had any positive slant to it. I became over-critical of myself. This started to rub off on my wife, and she started to lose confidence in the strength of our relationship. I think that I cut her out of this period of my life.

As I began to feel better, the depression gradually lifted and life started to feel better. I moved to a different department within the police and that made my life easier. People were not always asking after my health (something I hated) and I slowly started to put the event behind me.

The first anniversary of the fire was hard. It was in the news once again and I found my thoughts drifting back to the scene of the blaze. I got over that little setback, however, and life continues.

I think above everything else the event taught me a great deal about life. I now look more for the good in everything instead of looking at the bad side of things. I also count my blessings. I think of all the things I have, and I value them. Most of all, I value my family and friends. In a strange way the incident has brought us all closer together, we are more honest about our feelings and we have no secrets from each other.

Not only that, but this year I have been promoted!

1997 update: To get better it seems it is useful to have a move. It may just be geographical, or occupational or something else. This gets you away from the negative aspects of the trauma. It is not running away, it is a re-evaluation of your life. Do what you want to do most, and do it now because you just don't know what tomorrow will bring.

Because I was able to move, I have stayed with the job I have always enjoyed. I have a greater understanding of those who have been traumatised. Some of my colleagues call that being soft. It isn't, but they wouldn't understand if I tried to explain it to them. They are not part of the "trauma club".

I have heard that sometimes PTSD can end marriages, so perhaps I am lucky that the event appears to have strengthened my relationship with my wife. My wife is now my best friend too.

If I see a film or something on TV with a fire in the story then I sometimes have to walk away from the screen. It still triggers the memories but for the most part they are under control now.

CASE 8: ARLETTE

I was bullied. At the ripe old age of 52 I found myself struggling to cope with the way I was being treated by those around me. For ages I thought it was me. Then I realised that I was the victim in a situation over which I had no control.

1997 update: A psychologist wrote a report in which she stated that I was "subjected to heavy intimidation which culminated in Arlette taking sick leave followed by voluntary redundancy". That just about sums it up, except that even the psychologist was reluctant to use the word "bullied". I was out of a job before anyone began to take me seriously.

Of course now I am unemployed, it appears that everyone is willing to support my claims that I was being bullied. It makes me so angry that it all took so long. I feel that I need to take that anger out on someone and the victims of my temper are always those who are closest to me. I am going to have to be careful or I will end up with nothing.

I am now looking at a long and lengthy industrial tribunal in order to obtain compensation for my suffering. It was while gathering information for this tribunal that I was interviewed by a consultant psychologist from Harley Street and a psychiatrist. The conclusion was that I was suffering from Post Traumatic Stress Disorder type symptoms, and that I was probably suffering from Prolonged Duress Stress Disorder.

The tribunal date is now approaching and I am dreading it. However, I have found myself a few hours of teaching and I am really enjoying that. I think it will be some time before my life returns to anything like normal, but at least I can talk to others who have been bullied by contacting the National Workplace Bullying Advice Line.

CASE 9: FELICITY

Felicity is now in her final year at school. In the four years since she was first assaulted by her brother she has endured much. There is little doubt her story has been repeated in other family situations all around the world.

Soon after I told my friend's parents what had been happening I moved away from my parents and was fostered by a family in another county. I felt very tense and it was some time before I made any friends at my new school. When I did, they wanted to know why I had moved away from my parents and why I was living in a foster home.

I told them my mum was dead and my dad was in prison. That lie came easier than the truth.

In fact my parents kept in touch with me for a while. My brother still lived at home and they could not believe that what I was saying could possibly be true. They thought I had made it all up because I was jealous of my brother. I told them that it was impossible for me to come back home while my brother lived there and that if they didn't believe me that was their problem - not mine.

Sleeping was my problem. I hated to have the bedroom door shut, so it was agreed that I could leave it wide open every night. The trouble was I often had nightmares that woke up the rest of the household. My foster father would wake me, give me a drink and hope that I would fall back to sleep. I used to lie in bed and watch the clock during the early hours of the morning. No way could I get back to sleep.

One day at school we had a talk about drug abuse. A police woman gave the talk. I was sure that she knew I had been arrested for smoking stuff. At the end of the talk she looked right at me and smiled. I was convinced she knew all about me.

That night I didn't go back to my foster family. I walked for hours and was eventually picked up by a police car at 2 am. I sat in the back of the car terrified. They just took me back to my foster home though. They were all very nice and nobody shouted at me.

The next day, I told my foster mother about the talk at school and what I thought the police woman knew. She gave me a hug and made us a drink. She explained that she knew all about what had happened to me and that if I wanted to I could talk at any time. That was such a relief.

We talked on many occasions after that. It was great to have someone to talk to. Someone I could trust. My nightmares became less frequent and my school work started to improve. I got some good exam results, much to many people's surprise.

Occasionally I still feel a little awkward when anyone accidentally touches me or tries to hug me. It reminds me of my brother and all the horrible things in my past.

When I see pictures of children in other countries who are struggling to survive I still feel some kind of bond with them. It sounds silly, but I feel that I can appreciate and understand how they must be feeling. I know some girls have pictures of pop stars on their bedroom walls. In my bedroom I have a collection of Oxfam posters of children suffering in the poorest areas of the world.

I hope that my exam results will be good enough to get me a place at university next year. I'm still not sure what I want to do as a career, but I expect it will be something to do with children.

1997 update: Finishing my university course was a challenge. I nearly gave it up several times. But I stuck it out until the end and now I am about to start a teaching job that will help me repay my student loan. I am doing okay.

Okay is not brilliant. I don't have a boyfriend, but I do have friends. Perhaps I will never trust anyone enough to become really close. It is hard to explain in just a few words how I feel. It is just like there is a great slice of my life that I want to ignore - but I can't. When people start asking personal questions I just clam up or get moody with them.

I still sleep with the light on. Habit probably, but it is a comfort to do this. I never want to wake up in the dark again and as long as I can pay the electric bill there is no reason why I should. I hate power cuts! I hate going to the cinema too.

I suppose I am getting better. I just never think about it in those terms. I'm me, and that's all there is about it. Once or twice I have met up with small groups of people who have endured similar experiences and it helps. It helps but it hurts too.

I still keep in touch with the family that fostered me. They are great and they never ask questions. I've just moved and they helped me shift my stuff.

One thing that has been interesting me is Dolphin Therapy to help trauma sufferers. I have been following the research into this idea with a keen interest. Dolphins are such beautiful and relaxing creatures.

CASE 10: PAUL

Unlike the other victims in this book, Paul's trauma was well publicised by the media. It was a national disaster, and that factor added to the problems of recovery.

The week after the disaster was hell. There were pictures on the television and in the newspapers. Journalists were pestering for a good story. Nobody appeared to appreciate that I wanted to be on my own, and at home. In the end I went to stay with my parents in Surrey.

I was haunted by the memories of the incident. In just 60 seconds the ship went over, the lights went out and the water came in. Nearly 200 people died and I am sure I climbed over some of the bodies in order to save myself.

Physically and emotionally I was in a real state. I was suffering with tiredness, sleeplessness, bad dreams, loss of concentration, dizziness, shakes, muscular tension, headaches and backache. My broken arm gave me no real trouble.

I was visited by a social worker who said she was part of the 'away team' working with disaster victims. As I didn't live in Kent, I was being treated by her team. Although there were only 350 survivors of the disaster, my social worker said they were expecting to deal with around 10,000 people who had been affected in some way by the trauma. That included families and those involved in the rescue. This statement made me appreciate the scale of the event I had been caught up in.

After three weeks I returned to work. Everyone there wanted to know all the details. I found myself recounting my escape time after time. I made the story very unemotional - just as it was when I gave my statement. I left out the screams and the pushing and barging of frightened people clambering to get free.

One or two people saw through me, I think. They saw that there was more to it than I was telling.

The social worker became my counsellor and I saw her regularly. It was her idea that I should have more time off work, and my own doctor readily agreed to that. I simply couldn't concentrate on anything. I made lots of mistakes. My colleagues covered most of these for me, but I think they were relieved when I said I was having more time off.

At my parents' home, time dragged. The nightmares persisted and I started to shut everyone out of my life. I went on long walks, often just sitting on park benches and letting my thoughts drift back over the disaster.

I started to picture the faces of other people around me before the ship went over. I didn't know what had become of them. I started to feel guilty that I had survived while some of them had died. Then I felt ashamed of the fact that I may have climbed over their bodies to escape. I couldn't get these pictures out of my mind.

I'm not sure when I reached the lowest point after the disaster. It was about six weeks after the event I think. I thought I had flu. I just wanted to go to bed and die. My parents' doctor then pronounced that I was depressed and was suffering from Post Traumatic Stress Disorder.

It was such a relief to hear that I was normal, and that what I was experiencing was a normal reaction to an event that had almost killed me.

That knowledge helped me no end.

I could now see a point to the counselling. I was keen to tell everything - what I did, how I felt and what was worrying me. It was such a weight off my mind to be able to talk about it all. I stopped feeling ashamed.

I took five months off work. When I returned many things had changed but I was prepared for that. I had changed too. I worked steadily until the first anniversary of the disaster. That was a difficult time and I had to take a few weeks off again. Nobody seemed to mind that. They were very understanding.

I spent that time with my parents. We talked about the disaster. For the first time, we really talked about it. They told me about the news flashes. The horror when they realised that I was on the ship that was sinking - the ship they were watching on television. For the first time I was aware of the fact that they had been victims too. That sharing of knowledge brought us all much closer together.

It is all behind me now. I shall never forget it, but I can now live more easily with the memories. It was four years before I ventured onto a ship again. That was a big day for me. It was the final hurdle along my road to recovery.

1997 update: I was able to contact Paul, but he decided that he didn't wish to add anything to what he had previously written.

CASE 11: CHRISTINE

Christine was raped. She was raped by somebody she knew and respected. About 50 per cent of rape victims suffer PTSD symptoms. The experience affected not just Christine, but her family too.

By the time my husband and two daughters had returned home from their swimming session I had showered, cried, showered again, dressed and got halfway through my third brandy.

I told my husband that I'd had a row with one of the senior partners at work. I said my job was on the line and that I didn't really want to talk about it just now. I could see he didn't believe me, and I'd never lied to him before but I simply could not tell him the truth, yet. By the morning I would feel better. I had another shower before I went to bed.

The following day I phoned in sick. My head was splitting as a result of too much brandy. My legs were like jelly and I felt like a tramp. By 8.45 am I had the house to myself.

I couldn't stand being alone in the house. All my senses appeared to go into permanent alert as if the danger might return at any moment.

I worked my way through a whole packet of cigarettes and drank mugs of steaming coffee. Every time there was a noise in the house, I jumped out of my skin. By mid-afternoon I was a wreck. I went to the police.

During the next couple of weeks I had to undergo interviews and statement-taking that appeared endless. I had to tell my husband, and he was just great. Once he got over the initial desire to go around and thump the culprit he was wonderfully supportive to me. I had a medical examination and a pregnancy test. More questions to answer - then nothing. Week after week of nothing. It was as if everybody had forgotten the rape, except me. I still couldn't sleep, I kept seeing the inside of his room and that horrible smile of his. Our own lives resumed. Sex was difficult for me at first, but tender love and care from my husband eased my anxiety. God, how lucky I am to have him. During the day I became terribly irritable. My work suffered because I couldn't concentrate for long. I also had problems remembering things. I had to write down everything in my diary. I'd told my senior partner what had happened. He had trouble believing it, but went along with what I'd told him. It certainly explained the way my work had gone downhill. Then one day he asked me into his office. He said he had spoken to Dr xxxxx and that my story was a pack of lies. He'd been told that my attacker and I had been intimate on a number of occasions and that suddenly I'd had a change of heart about the relationship. I was horrified! That was my last day at work.

I became depressed and anxious about our family's financial situation. My company car had gone and I was going to find it difficult to find a similar job in such a rural area. Everything looked grim. It was my husband who found the solution. 'Leave things for a while and then set up on your own.' It sounded mad to start with, but the more I thought about it the better I liked the idea. It was what I had always wanted to do. The timing was forced upon us to some degree, but I had no doubt that I could make a success of things given half a chance and a few good clients. Looking back at things now, that was the turning point in my recovery. It is over two years now since I was raped. I have now been self-employed for just a couple of months as it took a while to get things organised. I work as much as my recovery permits me. We are not rich, but neither are we bankrupt. I still don't always sleep well, but that isn't too bad.

Recently, when my daughter caught me singing in the bath, she asked, 'Are you better now?' I wonder how much she understands about all this. The police dropped all charges and explained they were unlikely to get a prosecution. I thought I would be angry, but it was a relief in a way. I just want a chance to rebuild my own life again. I want to look to the future.

1997 update: Work-wise, things are going well and working for myself was the best thing I could have done. However, my marriage came to an end. It was a friendly break-up. We just wanted to do different things and held different values. Perhaps it would have happened anyway without the trauma of the rape. We will never know.

I have a new partner now. The only problem I have is when I am ill. I would do anything to avoid going to see my doctor, until my daughter pointed out that our new doctor was female. We both had a little laugh about that but I still don't enjoy going into the surgery.

We have not married yet, but are quite happy with the arrangement that we have. To be honest we behave like a couple of teenagers sometimes. The latest thing we have done together is to become naturists! Yes, I think I can honestly say that my memories are not interfering with my new life. Not very much anyway.

There are many features of these personal stories which are unique to the teller. On the other hand, there are a number of points that these victims have in common. Many of them talk about control. Being in control of our lives is so important to most of us and when you are involved in a traumatic event you lose that control. Regaining it can take a long time. Self-esteem is also important. Victims often have a very low level of self-esteem because they can no longer do the daily tasks that they took for granted. They become almost 'childlike' in their reliance upon other people to look after them. Rebuilding this self-esteem is something which needs to run alongside the regaining of control.

Chapter fifteen

Legal actions

The legal system can be an asset to victims of trauma in much the same way as therapists and friends. Victims turn to the legal system for redress from any physical or psychological injuries that have been inflicted on them.

Many victims will already have some general knowledge of the legal system, but there are experts in the field who are trained to help serve the needs of victims. Their title varies from country to country; in the USA the group is called VAP (Victim Assistance Programme) while in the UK a similar organisation is called Victim Support. Consult your local branch.

Some victims may turn to their own legal adviser for help.

After the disaster at Aberfan, no one sued for psychological shock, even though many parents not only lost their children but saw them dead. Following the Buffalo Creek disaster of 1972, lawyers started to examine the possibility of claiming compensation for psychological injuries. Prior to that, legal actions were restricted to claims for physical injuries and loss of earnings.

Compensation is not the primary worry of PTSD victims in the first instance. Immediately after any traumatic, potentially life-threatening event comes the trauma of making statements. Victims of motoring accidents are expected to make witness statements. Victims of assaults are expected to make a statement as an aggrieved party to the event.

Making a statement can be as traumatic as experiencing the event itself. There is a variety of views about how, and when, a statement should be taken. One school of thought is that any statement should be taken as soon after the event as possible. By doing this, the memories are as fresh as they can be and they are unlikely to be affected by other people's views of the incident (Joseph 1997).

The other viewpoint is that some people are not emotionally ready to think their way through the event and provide a statement for several days - maybe weeks. A few people may never feel able to provide a statement.

Statements are required for a variety of reasons: to establish that a crime or tort has been committed; to identify a guilty party; to provide evidence as to the precise cause of death of any victims. It follows, therefore, that the evidence obtained within a statement may be used at criminal proceedings, in civil courts and at inquests into the event.

The form that any proceedings will take depends on the country in which the event occurred. In instances where the event has occurred between international boundaries, at sea and in the air, the venue for any legal proceedings has to be mutually agreed according to international conventions. Whatever the location of proceedings there are some areas of common ground.

CRIMINAL PROCEEDINGS

Many physical and sexual assaults will result in criminal proceedings being taken against the assailant. As the victim of an assault, a PTSD sufferer is likely to be the primary prosecution witness. Even if the PTSD sufferer is a witness to the trauma, the existence of Post Traumatic Stress indicates that what the witness saw was fundamental to the case.

The matter does not end with the dictation of a witness statement. The victim may be asked to formally identify the accused. A second, or even third, statement may be needed. Eventually, a court appearance may be required.

Appearing in court requires careful preparation. It is a difficult and stressful ordeal for anyone. For a PTSD sufferer it can be very intimidating. Build up to the court date with your counsellor. Go through the event thoroughly, and restrict yourself to what you can remember. Try to block out what you have subsequently been told by others.

If possible, visit the court before the date of the trial and familiarise yourself with the surroundings. Knowing where the witness box is located in relation to the rest of the room will help you prepare for the occasion.

If it is all too much for you, discuss the matter with your doctor. If he agrees that attending court will adversely affect your condition he will provide the court with a letter to that effect. If this happens the court will either adjourn the hearing to a later date, or proceed without your verbal evidence. Clearly, your non-attendance may weaken the prosecution case, but if the trauma of the event has adversely affected your health once, there should be no reason for it to adversely affect your recovery, too.

At the end of the hearing, the issue is not over. Either side may appeal to a higher court if the outcome is not what they expected. Such an appeal may mean that you will have to go through the whole thing again.

For some years now, it has been acknowledged that rape victims have an arduous time at court; so merciless, that a large number of victims decline to attend court at all (Caruth 1995). What is true for rape victims is also true for a considerable number of victims of trauma, including bullying. Unfortunately, many courts fail to treat PTSD sufferers with the sympathy they deserve.

The procedure for criminal cases also applies to motoring offences which result in a court hearing. Witnesses and victims will be dragged through the same procedures.

CIVIL PROCEEDINGS

Cases which are brought before civil courts start in much the same way as criminal proceedings. There are two significant differences. First, the time span between the original event and the final court hearing is likely to be far greater in a civil case. It is not unlikely that the civil hearing will take three or more years to reach the court room.

Second, the level of proof required in a civil case is different from that required by criminal courts. Criminal courts demand that the case be proved beyond reasonable doubt. In civil courts the law demands that the case be proved on the balance of probabilities. In other words, if a person or company is 51 per cent to blame, that is enough for a civil court to prove the case.

Because of this difference in the level of proof required, civil proceedings tend to drag on and on as lawyers debate the issues they intend to present at court.

Some victims may find that they are the subject of an industrial tribunal. This may be so if you are the victim of bullying in the workplace, for example. One of the cases followed in this book is going to be settled by a tribunal.

Arlette:

The build-up to the case has been very stressful but I know if I want justice I just have to go through with it. Everything gets so personal. Medical evidence is there for all to see. I have also seen statements that are nothing but a pack of lies. If it wasn't for my family and their support, and the support of the National Workplace Bullying Advice Line I don't think I could continue with it all.

The built-in delays in civil proceedings may be seen as a blessing by those who are dreading the day that they have to attend court and give their evidence. However, the long delay can work against the victim's interests by dragging up past events, which have already been successfully dealt with during counselling sessions and filed away in the recesses of memory. In consequence, some people who had previously thought they had 'recovered' from the trauma may find some of the old symptoms recurring for a time. This would be a natural reaction, and one that witnesses should be prepared for.

INQUESTS AND INQUIRIES

Inquests are probably the most stressful proceedings to have to deal with. The investigation to verify why somebody died is always going to cause distress. It is necessary to hold an inquest, not only to establish a cause of death, but to look at the details of the incident and see that future incidents of the same nature can be avoided.

In those cases where there were no fatal injuries, an inquiry may be set up to work in the same way as an inquest, to try to prevent the trauma being repeated in the future.

Many victims of traumatic events have feelings of guilt. They feel guilty that they might not have acted correctly in the few seconds when the incident occurred. They feel guilty that they survived while others may have perished. They feel guilty for having survived. It is never easy to give evidence in court. To give your evidence while you have feelings of guilt can be very traumatic. These feelings should be worked through during counselling sessions before the court hearing. They are erroneous feelings which are one of the symptoms of Post Traumatic Stress. No matter what the situation, nobody has the right to criticise another person or anything they did, or didn't do, during a few seconds when they thought their own life was at risk. In 999 times out of 1,000 these feelings of guilt are unfounded. In the remaining cases they are unreasonable.

COMPENSATION

In the USA, since the Buffalo Creek disaster, the idea of Post Traumatic Stress Disorder has been accepted by the courts. It is now routine for disaster victims, whether they are survivors or the bereaved families, to receive substantial psychological damages running into millions of dollars.

In Europe, courts have been slower to accept this concept. Survivors of the Bradford Football Stadium Fire (1985) received no compensation for psychological damages. Passengers on The Herald of Free Enterprise (like Paul), which sank in 1987, had their claims for compensation finally settled by an arbitration panel. Paul received a fixed payment of £5,000 plus £5,000 for physical injuries and £24,000 for psychiatric injuries.

Many PTSD sufferers may find that they have a case for claiming compensation. How they set about making that claim will depend upon how their 'invisible injuries' were caused. However, the road to compensation is a long and winding one. The journey drags on for years and many sufferers decide to forget the whole thing and get on with the rest of their lives long before any offer of compensation is made. Others may, for the same reason, accept the first offer that is made - in order to put the experience behind them.

Whether or not to pursue compensation for your injuries is a personal decision. Do not make the decision too soon after the incident. The full impact of the trauma may not be apparent for several months. On the other hand, don't leave the decision too long. In many instances there is a time limit of three years, after which it is deemed too late to apply for compensation.

For many victims there is a legitimate desire for compensation. Because an injustice has been done to them they naturally feel entitled to some form of compensation. The quest for compensation is often an important part of recovery. At the same time, this quest may prevent sufferers from facing the full reality of what has happened to them. For many, there can be no adequate compensation.

The fact that police officers received compensation following the Hillsborough disaster of 1989 caused great distress to the family and friends of those who died. They held the police to blame for the incident, and yet here were certain officers being compensated. The award of £1.2 million shared between fourteen police officers was a landmark ruling. The awards were made in 1996, seven years after the disaster. Prior to these awards, the view had been that emergency service staff should not be compensated for simply doing their job. It must be remembered that awarding compensation, and attributing blame can be two different and complex issues. The compensation given to individual police officers did not necessarily mean that the police force was not is some way responsible for some of the wrong decisions taken at the time.

MEDICALS

Many people who are injured have to attend medical boards to be assessed as to their rate of recovery. This is true of PTSD sufferers too.

The assessment may be needed by your employer, or a government department, or a doctor wanting a second opinion. The medical results may be required by a court as evidence of your condition. Whatever the reason, many PTSD sufferers can expect to attend a string of medical examinations.

Now, if you had a broken leg or damaged hearing, it would be a simple task to examine you and assess how well your recovery was progressing. Because you are suffering from PTSD that assessment is far more tricky.

Medical examinations are often structured in the same way for every client. In consequence, the PTSD victim often attends a medical and is measured, weighed, and asked to provide a urine specimen.

Why? Because that is what it says on the form!

It may be a minor point, but a PTSD victim is not going to be impressed by a medical which begins with a urine sample. It suggests that those doing the assessment have no real idea of what PTSD is all about. If handled badly, such a medical can quickly degenerate into a battle between the patient and the doctor.

At these medicals, the examiners must trust the patient to tell them the truth about their condition. For months during treatment and counselling the sufferers have had to trust the counsellors and therapists. The medical is a time when the need for trust is reversed.

The only way a PTSD victim can be medically assessed is to be interviewed by someone qualified in the field of PTSD. The interview, or discussion, should be relaxed and as casual as possible. It should not feel like an interrogation, or like a cross-examination in the witness box. The patient should not feel as though he or she is on trial.

Many medicals which assess PTSD rely on the tests described in Chapter 10. By giving the patient a variety of tests it is relatively easy to assess the patient's progress. However, because of the nature of PTSD and any associated feelings of anxiety and depression, test results may vary, even from day to day.

PTSD AS A LEGAL DEFENCE

PTSD victims frequently suffer from flashbacks and from an exaggerated startle response. These two symptoms of the condition make them very 'jumpy' at times. It is hardly surprising therefore, that some PTSD victims have been guilty of crimes themselves. There have been instances of assault, robbery and even murder which, it is claimed, are indirect results of suffering from PTSD.

Marlene:

I learned about a combat veteran who heard a helicopter overhead in civilian life and had a flashback to the war itself. He stabbed a neighbour because he momentarily saw the neighbour as 'the enemy'. He was later convicted of assault.

There have been several instances where PTSD victims have reverted to their 'traumatised personality' and committed a crime which, a few moments later, they cannot even remember.

Matthew:

After the incident on the London Underground, I panicked for weeks. I knew I should not have hit the drunk, but I had no control over my actions for those few seconds. Luckily for me, I heard no more about the incident.

Cases such as these are coming before the courts more frequently. Each case must be treated on its own merits as courts struggle to interpret recent findings on human behaviour in a way that brings justice to both aggressor and aggrieved.

WARNING

Untreated victims of PTSD, or those who are not fully recovered, are prone to intrusive memories and sudden flashbacks of the traumatic event. Standing in a witness box, hostile cross-examination may act as a trigger to the body's emergency mobilisation systems and may cause the victim to re-experience the terror of the original traumatic event.

I attended court about ten months after my assault but I believe that the court hearing, and meeting my assailants face-to-face, pushed my recovery back many months.

Each PTSD sufferer must consider the issues involved in turning to the legal system for support. This is not in any way suggesting that the legal system should be avoided, but only that victims make informed choices about what to do. Courts can be helpful, but in many instances the rights of assailants still take precedence over the rights of the victim. Remember, courts have a duty to protect the innocent, but because of this duty innocent victims do not always receive justice.

Chapter sixteen

The future

Most books and reports on Post Traumatic Stress Disorder avoid looking into the future on behalf of PTSD victims. That is probably because the final chapter is by far the hardest to write.

Some people will make a swift and steady recovery. Many will recover in a series of stages, a long painful progress with milestones of both successes and failures. A handful may never fully recover, but their ability to cope with the symptoms will strengthen and grow as time passes. The human race has survived so far because people are adaptable. What PTSD does is to force change upon its victims too quickly - so time will heal.

To help illustrate different points in the text, eleven cases have been reported, with insights from the eleven adding to the general comments made. By way of conclusion, all were asked to comment on their present state of recovery and to use the snakes and ladders board as a guide to that recovery.

HAVE THE ELEVEN CASES RECOVERED?

David retired from the police 20 months after the incident and now writes for a living. Suffers with some symptoms occasionally. On square 97 in 1994. I now feel that I have leaped over the last snake to square 99.

Marlene left nursing to return to college, and is now a trained aromatherapist. On square 98 in 1994. She too has reached square 99. She had nothing further to add to her story in 2001.

Graham retired four and a half years after the incident and moved to Australia. Still has occasional feelings of depression. On square 95 in 1994. Graham slipped down to square 32 in August 1997, but with the help of his family has climbed back up again. I had a letter from him in 2001 saying that he was now at the top of the board.

Cindy is now married, and enjoying her work. She still refuses to drink alcohol. On square 99 in 1994. I was unable to contact her for an update in 1997, but she did phone over Christmas 2000 to confess that she no longer worried about snakes and ladders. I think we can take that as square 99. She also said that someone had identified her from reading this book - and that she saw that as a positive thing rather than something negative. She is very proud of her recovery.

Matthew, after three job changes, he has yet to settle. Life is still difficult. On square 75 in 1994 he had worked hard to reach square 92 three years later. Now he says he has finally reached square 99.

Jessica, late in diagnosis, it has been a struggle but the end is now in sight. On square 85 in 1994 she has now made good progress to square 96 and has just one snake to pass. She is now making plans for her daughter's twenty-first birthday party in 2002.

Richard, now promoted within the police after a change of duties. On square 99 in 1994 and is a little too cautious to admit that he has reached the final square. I think that he has just about got there.

Arlette has suffered badly from being bullied and I did not know her in 1994. Her industrial tribunal was imminent in 1997 and that placed her on square 79 which is one square away from a very long snake. With courage and help from her loved ones she leapt over that snake and in 2001 had reached square 96.

Felicity is still not finding it easy to form relationships, and still very much on her guard. On square 90 in 1994. She has successfully completed her university course since then and moved up to 96.

Paul has not made any comments since I last spoke to him in 1994 when he was on square 95 (the top of a snake). I don't know whether he has regained that ground yet, but we all hope so.

Christine was occasionally moody, but her move to self-employment is working out fine. On square 97 in 1994 she lost ground when her marriage ended (square 78) but has climbed back to square 94. In 2001 she claimed to have reached square 97.

It can be seen that those nearing full recovery are reluctant to claim they have finished the game and reached the last square on the board (100) but all have made progress. It is distressing to hear that Graham suffered such a major setback in 1997 but he is now positive about his recovery and the future. Remember, they all had to start at square one when they were traumatised.

The journey over the remaining squares may take many more months, or it may finish tomorrow. But the nearer each person gets to that final square, the fewer snakes lie in their path. Yes, this is a somewhat trivial way of assessing people's recovery from PTSD but nobody has yet devised a universally accepted alternative. At least everyone can understand what the snakes and ladders board is about.

All PTSD sufferers have experienced a traumatic, potentially life-threatening event or accumulation of events which need to be re-experienced in order to relate properly to each aspect of the trauma. You need to find out what frightened you.

The counselling process helps sufferers work through this trauma in much the same way as people need to grieve for a loved one who has died. At the end of any period of grieving, the person you loved is still dead. However, you have learned to cope with that death, that loss, and to rebuild your life without that person around you. Recovery from PTSD is much the same. You will never forget the trauma, but you will eventually rationalise the memory of the event so that you can think about it without having to relive it. Once you reach this stage of recovery you will have control over your past, rather than allowing your past experience to control you.

As with grieving, the turning point in recovery is reached when you realise that something in your life has changed permanently. You cannot turn the clock back and pray that the traumatic event never occurred. Its memory will remain and you have to master that memory.

It may be that you have to visit two or three counsellors before you meet a person you can openly discuss your situation with, someone with whom you feel most comfortable. Remember that counselling will raise painful issues for you. You must remind yourself not to drop out of treatment when the going gets tough. Too many PTSD sufferers fail to complete their treatment because the treatment has not been properly explained to them from the start. Ask questions of your counsellor.

During counselling, many sufferers take their thoughts back to their childhood. Memories which were presumed lost are rediscovered. The whole counselling process is a rediscovery of yourself. Because of what you have experienced, this discovery will be of a new self. Some childhood memories can be triggered by unusual sets of circumstances.

David:

I was in a convalescent home - it was about five months after my assault and I think my depression was at its worst. I had not tried to end my life, but I had thought about it for several days.

Then I opened a book that I had been lent. Inside I found a piece of poetry which I remembered hearing at some time during my childhood. It was written for Violette Szabo who was in the British resistance working in France during the Second World War. The poem was written by Leo Marks (and not Violette's husband, as I first thought) and Violette used it as her code key whilst working behind enemy lines. I had first heard the poem 26 years earlier when, as a child of nine, I watched the film, 'Carve Her Name with Pride'. I copied the poem onto a scrap of paper.

The life that I have,
   is all that I have.
The life that I have is yours.
The love that I have for the life that I have,
   Is yours and yours and yours.

~

A sleep I shall have,
   a rest I shall have.
Yet death will be but a pause.
For the peace of my years in the long green grass,
   Will be yours and yours and yours.

I kept that piece of paper in my pocket for months. Every time I felt low I would read it. I was amazed that I had remembered its significance in the film I had seen so long ago.

It gave me a strength. A strength to fight my way out of the depression I was in. I decided that many people had suffered far worse than I. I had not been held prisoner, tortured and shot, which was the fate of Violette Szabo.

Had I not rediscovered that childhood memory I don't think the discovery of that poem would have held any significance for me.

Many PTSD sufferers have explained how their experience has reshaped their way of life. It has given them a new set of priorities. There is also a strong view amongst those who have recovered from PTSD that they have a greater understanding of the problems of others. They can identify with the needs of other victims, and on many occasions former sufferers have turned counsellor and helped other victims overcome their fears.

Graham:

I find that my ideals and values of life have completely changed, for the better, may I add. Coming to terms with admitting that I was suffering from PTSD was one of the biggest hurdles, but once I'd accepted it things started to improve.

Many victims also have interesting comments on the subject of counselling, and sticking with it when it gets tough (something PTSD sufferers are not very good at).

Richard:

I suppose our minds automatically shut off when we are told something very unpleasant, and it is only when we are forced to face it that we have an understanding of what has happened.

Even those sufferers who feel they have made a good recovery from PTSD show an element of caution in their comments.

Cindy:

I still feel a bit wobbly on occasions. I'm sure this will go in time, and I really can't see me being as bad as I was - although, as they say, you have to be prepared for the odd setback. I have felt a bit dizzy on occasions (though it might be the start of a panic attack) but it hasn't developed into anything major and it

*definitely hasn't stopped me doing something I really wanted to
do.*

Looking at the positive side of Post Traumatic Stress
Disorder, the long recovery period gives ample time for reflection
and consideration of the future. This can, for a few, be a bleak
prospect, but with encouragement and guidance the future can
take on a positive air.

As a victim, you must be able to make sense of what has
happened to you in such a way that it allows you to continue with
the rest of your life. You have been unfairly treated by life's
fortunes. Consequently, you must devise a plan which hastens
recovery, restores self-esteem and provides a positive reason
for existence. Start to regard the bottle of life as being half-full,
not half-empty.

Playing snakes and ladders is different for every player.
Some make steady progress up the game board while others
rush ahead, only to land on a snake and be brought back down
the board. As the game nears its conclusion, players' tokens will
gather near the top of the board while they wait for the shake of
the dice that will give them the exact number required to finish
the game. One or two lucky players may shake that number at
the first roll of the dice. Some may spend long periods of time
waiting for the right number to fall, slowly edging nearer and
nearer to the 100 square. Eventually, every player will finish the
game, but some will have taken much longer than others. Those
of you who have played snakes and ladders will know that at the
start it is impossible to predict who will win, or how long the
game will take to play. Nobody can provide that information.

What is for sure, though, is that the longer you delay the start
of the game, the later in the day you will finish it. People with
Post Traumatic Stress Disorder get better because they're
tackling their problem and living with it. They have
acknowledged that the problem exists. They are not avoiding it.

From our early years we are told the old adage that every
cloud has a silver lining. Well, every silver lining has a price. You
have already paid the price, and your task now is to seek out the
silver lining. Remind yourself that it is possible to put your
experience behind you.

Since writing my first book, in 1994, I have become no stranger to the media and provided television and radio interviews promoting the plight of trauma victims. I have also been able to present workshops about PTSD to a large number of organisations, and at a variety of venues. I get great pleasure and satisfaction by running these workshops and it has been my own way of promoting the 'trauma bond' about which I feel so strongly. PTSD workshops have now become part of my new life. They have greatly assisted me in maintaining my own recovery and rebuilding my self-esteem. I trust they have also assisted those who attend as delegates.

There will come a time when you regain control of your past, and your past will no longer control you. That is recovery.

David Kinchin can be contacted to arrange a workshop. To make comments about his book:

email: david.kinchin@ntlworld.com

or by post, via Success Unlimited.

Bibliography and further reading

Alexander D et al, 2001, Ambulance personnel and critical incidents, British Journal of Psychiatry 178 pp 76-81

American Psychiatric Association, 1994, *Diagnostic & Statistical Manual of Mental Disorders (DSM-IV)*, Washington DC, American Psychiatric Association

Austin T, 1967, *Aberfan: The story of a disaster*, London, Hutchinson

Barnard P (Ed), 1998, *Children Bereavement, Trauma*, London, The Children's Society

Beitchman J H et al, 1992, A Review of the Long-Term Effects of Child Sexual Abuse, *Child Abuse & Neglect 16 pp101-118*

Blanchard E B et al, 1995, Short term follow up of post-traumatic stress symptoms in motor accident victims, *Behaviour Research & Therapy 33 pp 369-378*

Bradburn L S, 1991, After the Earth Shook: children's stress symptoms 6-8 months after a disaster, *Advances in Behavioural Research Therapy 13 pp 173-179*

Brewins C, 2001, A cognitive neuroscience account of posttraumatic stress disorder and treatment, *Behaviour Research & Therapy* 39 pp 373-393

Brown E, 1999, *Loss Change & Grief: an educational perspective*, London, David Fulton

Busuttil W, in press, The development of a 90 day residential program for the treatment of Complex PTSD. In *Innovative Trends in Trauma Treatment and Techniques* (Ed. Williams M B) Howarth Press, New York

Caruth C (Ed), 1995, *Trauma: explorations in memory*, London, John Hopkins

Cohen D, 1991, *Aftershock: the psychological and political consequences of disaster*, London, Paladin

Creighton S J, 1992, *Child Abuse trends in England and Wales 1988-1990, and an overview from 1973-1990*, London, NSPCC

Deblinger E et al, 1996, Sexually abused children suffering post-traumatic stress symptoms: initial treatment outcome findings, *Child Maltreatment 1 pp 310-321*

DeDomenigo G, 1982, Pain relief with Interferential Therapy, *Australian Journal of Physiotherapy 28: pp 14-18*

Deykin E Y, 1999, Postrraumatic Stress Disorder in Childhood and Adolescence: a review, *Medscapes Mental Health 4:4*

Dwivedi K N (Ed), 2000, *Post-Traumatic Stress Disorder in Children and Adolescents*, London, Whurr Publishers

Dyregrov A, 1998, Psychological Debriefing - An effective method?, *Traumatology e 4: 2 Article 1*

Dyregrov A, 2003, Early Intervention following Trauma, *Forum Vol 8 : 2*

Erikson K T, 1976, *Everything in its path: destruction of Community in Buffalo Creek flood*, New York, Simon & Schuster

Field T, 1996, *Bully in sight: how to predict, resist, challenge and combat workplace bullying*, Oxfordshire, Success Unlimited (see order form at back)

Flanney R B, 1992, *Post-traumatic Stress Disorder*, New York, Crossroad

Green B L et al, 1991, Children and disaster: Age, Gender and Parental Effects on PTSD symptoms, *Journal of the American Academy of Child and Adolescent Psychiatry 30 pp 945-951*

Herman J L, 1992, *Trauma and Recovery*, New York, Basic Books

Hetherington A, 2001, *The Use of Counselling Skills in the Emergency Services*, O U Press, Buckingham

HMSO, 1995, *Child protection: messages from research*, London, HMSO

Hoel H & Cooper C, 2001, Destructive Conflict and Bullying at Work, *Counselling at Work 32 pp 3 - 6*

Horowitz M J, 1979, Psychological response to serious life events. In V Hamilton & D Warburton (Eds) *Human Stress and cognition: an information processing approach*, New York, Wiley

James L et al, 1976, Family and character change at Buffalo Creek, *American Journal of Psychiatry 133:3 pp 295-299*

Joseph S et al, 1997, *Understanding Post-Traumatic Stress*, Chichester, Wiley

Keane T M, 1996, Clinical Perspectives on Stress, Traumatic Stress, and PTSD in Children and Adolescents, *Journal of School Psychology 34: 2 pp193-197*

Kinchin D, 1988, Fatal RTA: child involved, *Police Review 1/7/88 pp 1380-1381*

Kinchin D, 1992, Telophobia, *Nursing Times 88:52 pp 28-29*

Kinchin D, 1993, Heads in the sand, *Police Review Feb-1993*

Kinchin D, 1994, *Post Traumatic Stress Disorder: a practical guide to recovery*, Thorsons, London [superseded by this book]

Kinchin D, 1997, Post Traumatic Stress Disorder: aromatherapy and physiotherapy can be a prelude to effective counselling, *Alternative Therapies in Clinical Practice 4:2 pp 55-56*

Kinchin D, 1998 and 2001, *Post Traumatic Stress Disorder: the invisible injury*, Oxfordshire, Success Unlimited [superseded by this book]

Kinchin D & Brown E, 2001, *Supporting Children with Post-traumatic Stress Disorder*, David Fulton, London

Lacey G, 1972, Observations on Aberfan, *Journal of Psychosomatic Research 16 pp 257-260*

McLeer S V et al, 1992, Sexually abused children at high risk of post-traumatic stress disorder, *Journal of the Academy of Child & Adolescent Psychiatry 31 pp 857-879*

Malone C (Ed), 1996, *The Memory Bird: survivors of sexual abuse*, London, Virago

Marr N & Field T, 2001, *Bullycide: death at playtime, an exposé of child suicide caused by bullying*, Oxfordshire, Success Unlimited (see order form at back)

Mason P H C, 2000, PTSD and parenting, *The Post-Traumatic Gazette 6:1*

Mayou R et al, 1993, Psychiatric consequences of road traffic accidents, *BMJ 307 pp 647-651*

Meichenbaum D, 1997, *Treating Post-Traumatic Stress Disorder*, Chichester, Wiley

Miller J, 1974, *Aberfan: a disaster and its aftermath*, London, Constable

Mitchell J, 1993, CISD: an operations manual for CISD, defusing and other group crisis intervention services, Chevron Publishing Corp, Ellicott City

Mitchell M *et al*, 2000, Managing post incident reactions in the police service, HSE, London

Monahon C, 1993, *Children and Trauma*, San Francisco, Jossey-Bass

Napier M & Wheat K, *Recovering damages for psychiatric injury*, Blackstone Press

NSPCC, 1995, *Survey of childhood experiences: sexual abuse: summary*, London, NSPCC

Parker J & Randall P, 1997, Traumatic Stress Disorder and children of school age, *Educational Psychology in Practice 13:3 pp 197-203*

Parker J et al, 1995, Post-traumatic Stress symptoms in children and parents following a school-based fatality, *Child Care Health & Development 21:3 pp 183-189*

Parkinson F, 1997, *Critical Incident Debriefing*, Souvenir Press, London

Peggy T et al, 1998, Prevalence of Post Traumatic Stress Disorder and other Psychiatric Diagnoses in Three Groups of Children (Sexual, Physical, and both), *Child Abuse & Neglect 22:8 pp 759-774*

Raphael B, 1986, *When Disaster Strikes*, London, Unwin Hyman

Raphael B & Wilson J, 2000, *Psychological debriefing - theory practice and evidence*, Cambridge University Press, Cambridge

Rick J et al, 1998, *Workplace Trauma and its Management*, Norwich, HSE

Rose S, 2000, Evidence based practice will affect the way we work, *Counselling 12:2 pp 105-107*

Scott M J & Stradling S, 1992, *Counselling for Post-Traumatic Stress Disorder*, London, Sage

Scott M J & Palmer S, 2000, *Trauma and Post-traumatic Stress Disorder*, London, Cassell

Stallard P & Law P, 1994, The Psychological effects of traumas on children, *Children and Society 8:2 pp 89-97*

Stern G M, 1976, *The Buffalo Creek Disaster*, New York, Vintage Books

Tehrani et al, 2002, *Psychological debriefing - Professional Practice Board Working Party*, British Psychological Society, Leicester

Terr L C, 1981, Psychic Trauma in Children: observations following the Chowchilla school-bus kidnapping, *American Journal of Psychiatry 138:1 pp 14-19*

Terr L C, 1983, Chowchilla revisited: the effects of psychic trauma four years after a school-bus kidnapping, *American Journal of Psychiatry 140:12 pp 1543-1550*

Turnbull G, 2003, The Biology of PTSD, Presentation to Sunderland Counselling Services 9/2003

Yule W et al, 1990, Post-Traumatic Stress reactions in Children, *Journal of Traumatic Stress 3:3 pp 279-295*

Yule W & Udwin O, 1991, Screening child survivors for post-traumatic stress disorders: experiences from the 'Jupiter' sinking, *British Journal of Clinical Psychology 30 pp 131-138*

Yule W & Gold A, 1993, *Wise before the Event: coping with crises in schools*, London, Calouste Gulbenkian Foundation

Yule W, 1999, *Post-Traumatic Stress Disorder: concepts and theory*, Chichester: Wiley

References from the Internet

Hamblen J, 1998, PTSD in Children and Adolescents, www.ncptsd.org/facts/

Goguen C, 1999, The Effects of Community Violence on Children and Adolescents, www.ncptsd.org/facts/

Jankowsi K, 2000, PTSD and Physical Health, www.ncptsd.org/facts/

Buckley T, 1999, Traumatic Stress and Motor Vehicle Accidents, www.ncptsd.org/facts/

Catherall D, 1999, Secondary Stress and the Professional Helper, www.ctsn-rcst.ca/

Hambling J, 1997, On the Efficacy of CISD, www.ozemail.com.au/

Hambling J, 1996, Tipping the Scales in the Debriefing Debate, www.ozemail.com.au/

Whealin J, 1999, Child Sexual Abuse, www.ncptsd.org/facts/

National Center for PTSD, 2000, PTSD and The Family, www.ncptsd.org/facts/

Greenwald R, 1999, Trauma Information for Parents, http://childtrauma.com/

Greenwald R, 1999, When it's too late to 'be careful', http://childtrauma.com/

Jaksec C M et al, 2000, Classroom Teacher's Ratings of Acceptability on in-class crisis intervention services, Traumatology e 6:1 art 2, www.fsu.edu/~trauma/

Straton D S, 1999, The Trouble with PTSD, Traumatology e 5:1 art 4, www.fsu.edu/~trauma/

Puffer M K et al, 1998, A single session EMDR study with 20 traumatised children and adolescents, Traumatology e 3:2 art 6, www.fsu.edu/~trauma/

Web Pages of interest

UK

Nottingham Trent University, Centre for Traumatic Stress,
http://ess.ntu.ac.uk/trauma

Bully OnLine trauma pages,
www.bullyonline.org/stress/ptsd.htm

Canada

Canadian Traumatic Stress Network, www.ctsn.org

USA

International Society for Traumatic Stress Studies, www.istss.org

Mental Health Net, http://mentalhelp.net/

Child Trauma Home Page, http://childtrauma.com/

American Psychiatric Association, www.psych.org

Florida State University - "Traumatology e",
www.fsu.edu/~trauma/

National Center for PTSD, 2000, Complex PTSD,
www.ncptsd.org/facts/specific/fs_complex_ptsd.html

National Center for PTSD, www.dartmouth.edu/dms/ptsd

Organisations

ASSIST, 11 Albert Street, Rugby, Warwickshire CV21 2RX, UK
Tel 01788 560800

TACT, Buttfields, The Farthings, Withington, Gloucestershire
GL54 4DF, UK, Tel 01242 890306

Index

Post Traumatic Stress Disorder

Comments and feedback

Email:
 david.kinchin@ntlworld.com

Or post to:
 Success Unlimited
 PO Box 67
 Didcot
 Oxfordshire OX11 9YS
 UK

Post Traumatic Stress Disorder

Order Form

Please send me .... copies of David Kinchin's
POST TRAUMATIC STRESS DISORDER: THE INVISIBLE INJURY, 2005 ED
at **£16** a copy UK (rest of Europe £17.50, outside Europe £18.50)

Please send me .... signed copies of Tim Field's
**BULLY IN SIGHT: HOW TO PREDICT, RESIST, CHALLENGE AND
COMBAT WORKPLACE BULLYING** at **£18.95** per copy in the UK,
(rest of Europe £19.90, outside Europe £22.15)

Please send me .... copies of Neil Marr and Tim Field's
BULLYCIDE: DEATH AT PLAYTIME at **£16.50** per copy in the UK,
(rest of Europe £17.50, outside Europe £19.95)

Prices include postage & packing. 30-day money-back guarantee.

Name (BLOCK LETTERS) ....

Address ....

....

....

Postcode ....

☐ I enclose sterling cheque payable to "Success Unlimited"
or credit card: Visa ☐ MasterCard ☐ Switch/Maestro ☐

Card number ....

Switch/Maestro issue number ....

Expiry date ....

Name on card ....

Signature ....

**Send to: Success Unlimited, PO Box 67, Didcot,
Oxfordshire OX11 9YS, UK**
**Order online at
www.successunlimited.co.uk/books/**
Telephone orders: 0700-ACHIEVE (2244383)
Trade enquiries welcome